At the Heart of it All

· AN AUTOBIOGRAPHY ·

Frances Clarke

Published by VIRAGO PRESS Limited 1993
20–23 Mandela Street, Camden Town, London NW1 OHQ

Copyright © Frances Clarke 1993

All right of Frances Clarke to be identified as the
author of this work has been asserted by her in accordance
with the Copyright, Designs and Patents Act 1988

*A CIP catalogue record for this book is available
from the British Library.*

Typeset by Florencetype Ltd, Kewstoke Avon
Printed in Great Britain by Cox
Wyman Ltd, Reading, Berkshire

I should like to extend my sincere thanks to everyone at
Virago Press, especially Lynn Knight, whom I now regard as a
friend, and without whose help this book would never have
been written. That's said at the beginning of every book,
but in this instance it's perfectly true. She guided me and
gave me confidence and support when I was ready to
throw my hand in.

This book is for my best and dearest friend Rene Rowe, who passed away on April 30th 1993, and whose strong influence on my life shows in these pages. She was a woman who dedicated her life to the benefit of others for no financial reward; she was a fighter against bigotry, inequality and any form of discrimination. Her generosity was her trade mark. Rene was not religious but she loved her fellow human beings and I pray that she rests in peace.

Contents

List of illustrations

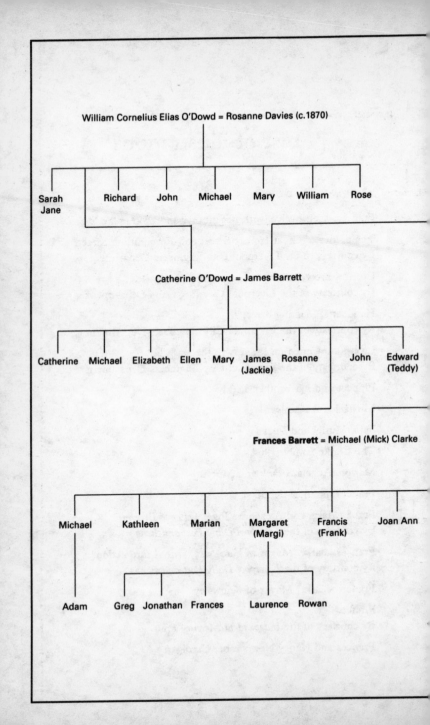

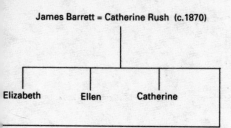

James Barrett = Catherine Rush (c.1870)

- Elizabeth
- Ellen
- Catherine

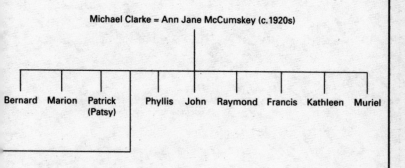

Michael Clarke = Ann Jane McCumskey (c.1920s)

- Bernard
- Marion
- Patrick (Patsy)
- Phyllis
- John
- Raymond
- Francis
- Kathleen
- Muriel

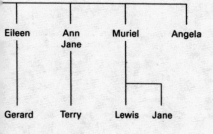

- Eileen
- Ann Jane
- Muriel
- Angela

- Gerard
- Terry
- Lewis
- Jane

· 1 ·

Family History and
Childhood Tales

I was born in Liverpool in 1929, the year of the Wall Street Crash, which seems appropriate, as I was going to make a bit of a splash when I grew older. In my life, just like everyone else's, there have been some funny episodes and some extremely sad ones, too – although my family seems to have acquired a degree of notoriety. My story is also that of the working-class community that has shaped me and, like all family histories, it began before my time.

My grandfather, William Cornelius O'Dowd, came from Southern Ireland, near Wexford, but his family moved to Liverpool in the 1800s. There he met and married Rosanne Davis, whose parents hailed from the slate quarries of North Wales. Billy was a lovely man, small but fiercely independent. He was a seafarer, but after his marriage he worked on the docks. He and Rosanne lived all over Liverpool. We used to say to Ma, 'You must have been gypsies, always on the move from one place to the next,' but I reckon they had to keep one step ahead of the landlord. Times were hard for them and it was nigh-on impossible to make ends meet, but they maintained their dignity in whatever ways they could: it was my grandmother's proudest boast that they had fresh straw for their beds every day. In those days mattresses were filled with straw – 'the donkey's breakfast'.

Grandma used to take in washing. Her nickname was Mrs Happy, because she was always laughing and singing. She was also a hawker, selling fruit and vegetables from a handcart. As the eldest of their large family, my Aunt Sarah and my mam, Catherine, used to help her. Like most working-class kids, they had to do their share to bring money into the household.

There was a knack to selling, and although Mam liked selling vegetables, and was good at it, she hated dealing with fish. When money was particularly tight, Grandma would go down to Liverpool's fish market and buy six penn'orth of herrings – she'd get about two dozen for that. She'd wash, bone and roll the herrings, then lay them out on white paper in a basket. Whoever was in the house had the job of taking them out to sell. Mam got caught one day.

'Catherine, come on now, out you go with these herrings.'

'Oh Mammie, I'd much rather take a box of bananas' – but her mother insisted.

'I haven't got any money for bananas, so you'll have to sell these.'

Mam was about eleven at the time, and she wasn't a bit happy with the idea.

In those days many women carried their shopping

and laundry in baskets on their heads, and the women who sold from baskets were known as 'Mary Ellens'. Mam had lovely curly jet-black hair, and to protect it and provide a base for the basket, she'd tie up a length of towel or a piece of sheet and twist it into a ring. With that on her head, she'd walk down the street with her wares. Mam was only five foot two, and Dad used to say that it was the weight of the basket that kept her so small. On this occasion, she was going down the street when she spotted a policeman. As you weren't supposed to sell anything without a licence, she was panic-stricken and started walking faster. The police-man quickened his pace as well. When he caught up with her he said, 'Come here, little girl, you'd better get these fish back home to your mother.' There was a hole in the basket, and the faster she'd walked, the more fish she'd lost. The policeman had been picking them up.

My grandparents had their share of woe: one of their children was killed in an accident; another died in the First World War. Grandma herself was only forty-two when she died. Fortunately, she never knew what happened to her youngest children. Willie and Mary were very young when their mother died, and although Billy tried to do his best for his family, Willie and Mary were always playing truant. That was considered a very serious offence in those days and the authorities decided that they should be sent away to populate the colonies. Mary was twelve and Willie was eleven.

My grandfather was uneducated, and didn't know who to turn to. Consequently, Mary and Willie were sent to Canada. Just imagine that: you're only a child, you know no one else on the boat, and you see your father and your other brothers and sisters standing on the quayside, crying because you're going away, and you know in your heart and soul that it's unlikely you'll ever see them again.

For the rest of the family, it was just as if they'd died; the ones left behind were heartbroken as well. My mother corresponded with Mary and Willie over the years. I don't know what happened to them in their youth, but later they lived in Montreal, and both married and had children. I think that Willie's family are still there, and that Mary's moved to Vancouver.

That was the State removing children from their families without taking their thoughts and feelings into account. They weren't little tearaways – though even if they were, they deserved to have a better life meted out to them, not to be deprived of their family. The anguish parents felt must have been unbelievable. What a heartless system.

The family moved to Portland Place. My dad, James Barrett, lived nearby, in Roscommon Street. He was an only son with four sisters, and liked to be in charge: no one was going to get the better of him. After tea, especially in the summer, the girls of the neighbourhood would sit at the corner of the nearby courtyard and watch the world go by. Dad would walk by and say, 'Hello, curly head!' to Mam, who'd smile. That was their first introduction. I don't think I ever heard him use another term of endearment to her: he wasn't a man who showed his emotions. Someone else took a shine to Mam – a boss at Tate & Lyle, called Charlie – but when Dad got wind of that, Charlie was seen off with no hesitation.

My parents married in 1913. My father wasn't very domestic; he was a man's man, and had a reputation for being outspoken – no one dared cross him. I think if anyone had challenged him, they'd have won, because I don't think he was a fighter, but his manner was tough, and no one ever risked it. He went away to sea for a while, then he was called up for the Army. After the 1914–18 war he was determined that he wasn't going to be pushed around any longer, and taught himself to be a ticktack man at the races. It was a job that gave him quite a bit of freedom – he'd go to racecourses all over the country. The bookie he worked for must have thought highly of him, because he supplied him with several good suits. Dad always looked the part.

My mother had ten children, six girls and four boys, and I was the eighth to arrive. We lived on Roscommon Street, in a large Georgian house that had originally been built for a Liverpool merchant. By the time we lived there, it was pretty dilapidated; its days of grandeur had passed. We shared the building with another family, the McCullochs and their four children. They lived on the first floor, in two rooms, but we were more fortunate, with a kitchen and a front room on the ground floor and three bedrooms upstairs. Even so, it was a bit of a squash with ten children, and we slept three to a bed. There was gaslight downstairs but only candles upstairs, so the McCullochs only ever had candlelight. In the yard there was a lavatory and a standpipe for our water. We took our laundry to the public wash-house, and if we wanted a bath we generally went to the public one. Of course we had a tin bath, but the business of heating up water from the outside tap in pots and pans didn't make that very tempting. In the basement of the building was the cellar, a gloomy, damp place, long since disused. I remember standing at the window as a small child and seeing four rats coming up the cellar steps towards our door. I was petrified, and the fear of rats has stayed with me to this day.

Roscommon Street was like a village. At the top was the demarcation line of the Orange Order. When 12 July came, they'd all be out celebrating; on 17 March Mam and the other Catholics would be doing just the same. At times, the antagonism between Catholics and Protestants in the neighbourhood was terrible, but all bitterness was put aside for those two days. Fortunately, not everyone was hostile; after all, whatever our religion, we shared the same difficult, poor circumstances.

I thought Roscommon Street was fabulous. Its shops sold everything from a pin to a battleship and it had two cinemas, to which I was a frequent visitor. There was a row of stables where farmers and circus people brought their animals, and I'd watch all the huge Shire horses going in and out and being led to the veterinary surgeon further down the road. It was a wonderful sight for a small girl. There was a pub, and a fish 'n' chip shop, and the street boasted 'Mary Cosgrove's Cooked Dinners'. Mary sold roast potatoes, meat, vegetables and cakes – you went along with your own plate and took the food home. As far as I'm concerned, that was the first ever takeaway in Liverpool. You could also hire a bike for a penny an hour from Mr Mackie. I always wanted my own bike – though I never got one – so I loved going there. I remember falling off one of his boneshakers and spraining my wrist and God knows what else . . .

We children had our favourite sweet shops. I liked Lily Ambers's – she wore long old-fashioned clothes, and her husband had a starched collar and a moustache. Every Sunday they'd go out in a horse and carriage, and they were the envy of the neighbourhood. I also liked Miss Bentham, who was very friendly and kind. She once took me behind her counter – a great honour – and bandaged my sore finger. When we'd decided which shop we favoured, we joined a sweet club, paying a halfpenny a week – or whenever we had a halfpenny to spare – from the summer through to Christmas. A shilling bought a selection box. I was rather greedy, and decided that I would save half a crown for the largest Cadbury's sweet club on sale. I put all my halfpennies and pennies together for this, and as there was to be a raffle as well, I also bought a ticket. Christmas came, and I collected my huge selection box. What's more, I won first prize in the raffle – another half-crown box of chocolates. I wouldn't give anyone else any sweets, but I paid the price for my greed. I was *so* sick.

Like her mother before her, Mam went out with a handcart. Whatever the weather, she'd be working. The handcart itself was a large heavy wooden crate with a wheel at either side. It could hold pounds and pounds of fruit and vegetables, and with high boards placed within each side, they could be piled high: it was like a small market stall on wheels. There'd be sprouts, potatoes, three dozen cabbages, onions and everything, and with a box of bananas on the handle shafts and probably a basket of flowers dangling from them, Mam would be ready for off. It's just as well that although she was short, she was quite stout: her living required a great deal of stamina.

When I was a toddler I sometimes used to sit at the front of the handcart in a fruit box, and on the way home I'd snuggle into her arms and she'd wrap me up in the big grey Irish shawl she used to wear, with its decorative fringing hanging down. As I got older, I'd walk with her. I enjoyed listening to all the people we met, but I didn't like being asked to help her sell things, as I didn't enjoy drawing attention to myself.

'Here y'are, girl,' she'd say. 'Go and stand on the corner with these bunches of mint.'

'I'm not asking.'

'Well, how are people going to know that you're selling, if you don't ask if they want to buy, or you don't say "Tuppence a bunch of mint"?'

'I'm not doing that.'

I did, of course, but I was as reluctant as Mam had been with the herrings when she was a child.

Mam would push the cart to Bootle, eight or ten miles away, and bring it back at night. The people of Bootle held her in high regard because they recognised her as a hard worker who tried to give them a bargain if she could. But she had to keep her wits about her. Money was scarce by the middle of the week, and many people took food on trust. On Fridays, when their husbands got paid, there'd be a few wise Herberts who'd avoid her. Mam needed to recoup the money because she'd borrowed it to buy the vegetables in the first place. Her priority had to be the interest she owed to the moneylender. Anything she made beyond that was her own profit, but sometimes that profit disappeared through her own good nature. She wasn't prepared to see young women with babies go without food, so she always gave trust.

Most people repaid her, and they repaid her with loyalty on top. Lots of women waited for her cart in particular, and some of them made sure that she had a hot meal. 'Here y'are, Catherine,' they'd say, offering jugs of tea and something to eat. They looked after her well, and knew they could rely on her.

She bought all her produce from the North Market, which had earned its place in history during the 1911 police strike. Shops were looted and windows were smashed, and a battalion was dispatched to Liverpool and ordered to fire on the crowd. However, many of the soldiers were local men, and refused. Charged with mutiny, they were put under close arrest in the market. People came from all over the city and marched round the boundary, throwing sweets and tobacco to the troops. Many of their brothers and sons were involved, and ours has always been a community that sticks together.

The troops had become a local memory by the time Mam visited the market. She had to be there for about six o'clock in the morning to begin the daily bargaining. The market was near to Roscommon Street, and sometimes I joined her later – you wouldn't get me out of bed at that hour – and looked at the covered wagons and horses, and sat among the noise and the bustle, listening to Mam trading with the farmers. If there was a glut of a particular vegetable, she bartered to knock the price down. Then she told another hawker, and the word would spread from one woman to another, so that everyone could benefit. This was the way the traders lived, helping one another to get the best deal rather than competing. They all worked extraordinarily hard; sometimes they drank, and sometimes their drinking became a problem – but Mam couldn't afford to drink: she had too much work to do and too many children to look after, and with my dad here, there and everywhere at the races, it was all left on her shoulders.

On Saturdays she didn't get home until about ten o'clock at night, and then she cooked me something to eat. I'd been left in the care of Mary and Nellie, my older sisters, but I refused to go to bed until Mam came back. Despite being out all hours, she kept the house spotless, and although she must have been exhausted, she never complained. It didn't matter what happened, she kept on working, even through tragedy. My sister Rose and my brother John were only two or three years old when they died, but I can see Mam now, brushing out the kitchen, which had a lovely blazing fire, and crying about John as she swept. I remember clinging to her pinny, saying, 'Don't cry, Ma, don't cry.'

When I was five I developed a large abscess on my head, and Mam took me to the homeopathic hospital.

All the poorer people used to go there because homeopathic medicines were the only ones they could afford. It was rather like a medical centre: they diagnosed illnesses, and prescribed, and treated emergencies, but you couldn't stay overnight. The doctor said I was too ill to be taken home, and should go to the main hospital. I remember Mam and our Lizzie taking me there. I knew something was up, and I was a real terror on the way, so Mam stopped a hawker and bought some bananas to pacify me. I was having none of it; I wasn't going to be bought for anyone.

I remember it all to this day, especially the nurse and my absolute terror when she took me from my mother. Mam stood crying, and our Lizzie was crying, and saying, 'She'll be all right, she'll be all right.' I was taken into the admissions room – there was a bath in the middle. I didn't want to get into it, and I didn't want anyone else to take my clothes off. I was a very private child, and I wasn't going to allow anyone to undress me. I kicked up blue murder, but somehow they got me into that bath.

I was taken to a ward with French windows, and as soon as someone opened them, I saw my opportunity to escape. I was out of bed in an instant, and ran like the wind across the lawn. One of the nurses spotted me, came running after me, and brought me back. As I was hysterical, they tied me to the bed. Looking back on it, I realise they did this to prevent me from damaging myself, or running out of the grounds and into the road, but I was terrified. I was so devastated that they stopped my mother and father from coming to see me because it upset me so much when I couldn't leave with them. I was in hospital for only a couple of weeks, but it seemed like a lifetime. I hated it so much that while I was there, I would do things that cut off my nose to spite my face.

There was a concert, and a nurse said, 'Come on, Frances, we'll take you,' but I refused to go. I desperately wanted to go, but I was determined that I wasn't going to give in to them; there was no way I was going to be happy in that hospital. All I wanted to do was go home. No matter what they did to coax me, or try to win me over, I wasn't having any of it. I was an obnoxious little kid.

When I was almost ready to go home, my dad came in to see me. I was absolutely delighted. I'd thought that I'd been abandoned, and the little girl I'd made friends with was an orphan, which made my fears worse. I was over the moon when I saw him, and of course I wouldn't let him go. Wherever he went, I went.

He'd brought me lots of fruit, and towards the end of his visit, he said, 'Who's your friend over there?'

'Her name's Emily Finn, and do you know what, Dad? She lives in the Cottage Homes, and she gets steam flies in her pudding.'

'Here y'are, go and give her this orange,' he said.

He thought that by the time I'd reached the other side of the ward and given the orange to Emily, he'd be able to make his getaway. But I had him sussed, so I said 'OK' and shouted, 'Emily!' Emily turned round, and I threw the orange to her. I'd foiled his scheme.

Shortly afterwards, my dad said, 'Look, daughter, I've just got to go to the lavatory. Where is it?' He spoke so convincingly that I told him. As soon as he'd gone,

I realised what I'd done. I was absolutely distraught. Nowadays, if any child goes into hospital, I want their mother or someone else in the family to be with them, so that they don't feel abandoned, like I did.

When Mam came to take me home, she brought me a pair of black patent ankle-belt shoes, white socks, a pleated skirt with a bodice, and a red jumper. I can't describe how excited I felt when I walked up that long corridor with her. It was heaven. Back home, I was the centre of attention, but I was heartbroken about my hair. Because of infection it had all been cut off, and I was very sensitive about it. My brothers and sisters teased me, children in the street teased me, and I started to cry. I took to wearing a hat, and I wouldn't go anywhere without it. It would have been all right if the hat was a little bonnet, but oh no, it was a large-brimmed velour hat – not quite as big as the one Hos Cartwright of *Bonanza* wore, but not far short of it.

Because I was so upset, Mam wanted to find ways to please me and keep me quiet, so when I said, 'I want to do the step,' she said, 'All right, girl.' Everyone cleaned their step with sandstone, and drew a line at the edge as decoration. When you think back, we must have all been crackers, kneeling outside, doing our front step to perfection. Mam kitted me out with a bucket of water, a floorcloth, a brush and sandstone, and the whole of Roscommon Street saw a little girl in her apron scrubbing the steps, almost hidden by the great big hat on her head. I must have looked a picture.

In the same year I started school at All Souls, the parish school in Collingwood Street. I loved school, although it was a shame that few of the teachers really made me feel that I was intelligent and had potential. The headmistress of the Infants, Sister Margaret, taught religious education in preparation for our First Holy Communion at the age of seven. She was known for being a strict disciplinarian, and would swoop on our pronunciation:

'Don't sing "O Sacrament Most Holy", it's got to be "O Sarcrament Most Holy", and don't make it woolly.'

My First Holy Communion was the highlight of my life – I think it's the highlight for any child within the Catholic religion. The preparation was intense. Priests tested our knowledge of the faith, and when they were satisfied, we took Communion. Our mothers were asked to buy a dress, a veil and a wreath for this special occasion. Some parents couldn't afford veils and wreaths, and their children wore white berets; I did, and I was disappointed. I wanted a wreath and a veil, and outstanding ones at that, but it was not to be. The ceremony took place on a Saturday morning – a busy time for Mam, who couldn't come, but my sisters Lizzie, Mary and Nellie came, and they made me feel as if I was the one that day.

We children looked lovely – whether we wore a wreath and veil or not – but being who I am, I didn't think to take off my dress after the celebration party at school. I wanted to go out and show off; I wanted people to say, 'Oh look, isn't that little girl gorgeous!' So I went to the park to play on the maypole, which didn't do much for my white clothes.

I loved any occasion that gave me an excuse to put on my best dress and enjoy a bit of singing and dancing, and when my parents decided that they were going to have a do – no one ever said they were having a party, it was always a do – for Catherine, my eldest sister, when she came of age, I was thrilled by the prospect. She was fifteen years older than me, very much a grown-up, and we younger ones always took notice of whatever she told us. I knew that her twenty-first birthday party would be something special.

Mam and Catherine went to the brewery in Soho Street to order the ale, and I insisted on going with them, even though a brewery was hardly the place for a small girl. Wherever they went, I had to go and, discretion being the better part of valour, they thought it better to take me with them than to have me pursuing them, screaming, down the street. They ordered a barrel of bitter and one of mild – an unbelievable purchase for a working-class family in 1935. When the barrels were delivered, we all stood admiring them, though someone got a belt off my dad for leaving one of the beer taps running when he'd paid so much precious money for it. He didn't mind the beer disappearing down someone's throat, but he certainly wasn't going to see it go to waste.

On Catherine's birthday, all the girls from the neighbourhood started to arrive in their long dresses; they looked lovely, completely transformed by their best clothes. Just as people were gathering at the house, Mam sent me to fetch my auntie Rosie. She lived in Titchbourne Terrace – a pretty good hike for a six-year-old. At first I refused to go because I didn't want to miss anything, but they assured me that the party would wait for my return. When I reached Auntie Rosie's I gave her the message, then turned on my heel and rushed back home. At Roscommon Street my parents screamed blue murder because I hadn't waited for Auntie. Mam said that they'd put some food to one side for me, but it just wasn't the same. I'd wanted to be in at the kill, not arrive out of breath to find a party in full swing. Catherine had been given a piano for her birthday, and this was the centre of attention. Family and friends were grouped around it, playing their party pieces. Our Mary was the star performer, but I was allowed to try out a tune, and at least my little tinkle on the keys cheered me up.

In 1936, at the age of eighteen, our Lizzie married Billy Pringle. My dad was strict with all of us; he kept an eagle eye on the lads who came calling for his daughters – he saw off one or two of them – and was especially firm about the hour we were due in. During their courtship, Lizzie made all kinds of excuses when she arrived home late. She'd seen a fire, or an ambulance, arrive at someone's doorstep – there was no end to the excuses she concocted when, of course, she was out with Billy all the time. One evening my dad spotted them together and called them every name under the sun, threatening them both with God knows what he was going to do when he got hold of them. Billy was a young man of twenty or twenty-one, and if he'd turned round to my dad, he'd have blown him away, but fortunately he kept his temper for our Lizzie's sake.

Dad's rage cooled, and Lizzie announced that she was going to get married.

That was a day to remember. The wedding took place at All Souls', but as Billy was a Protestant they couldn't marry at the altar, so the ceremony took place in the vestry. They had to promise that their children would be brought up in the Catholic religion, but I don't think Billy was too bothered about that because he was so besotted with Lizzie. She was lovely to look at, with shining auburn hair, and had a very outgoing personality. In fact, our Margi's something like her. Lizzie had a lovely bouquet and wore a salmon-pink velvet dress; she looked like a princess to me. I was asked to collect the flowers from home and take them to the vestry. It seemed to me that I was about to miss out on yet another event, but as they bribed me with tuppence, I did as I was told. The celebrations went on for days. It was wonderful, and all for our Lizzie. She deserved it.

When I was seven I moved up to the 'big girls' school' at the top of the building. There I met Miss Murphy, a teacher who had a great influence on my life. She was an excellent teacher, although she was quite a tartar at times. She also put personal hygiene and appearance at the top of her priorities. Every morning we had to stand before her, with our hands out, then turn them over to show that we'd been washed and our fingernails were clean. If we passed her scrutiny we got a point, and the one with the most points at the end of each week received a prize. That kept us on our toes.

I always tried to impress Miss Murphy, but I always failed. I sat in the back row and played silly games with the girl who sat next to me. She didn't seem to get caught, but I did. I was always puzzled how Miss Murphy knew who was talking when she was facing the blackboard – I didn't realise that she could see the reflection through her glasses. I was hauled out in front of the class for the cane, but I never cried; it was a battle of wills between us. I wasn't a bad child, I was just exuberant and a chatterbox. Although there were lots of subjects that I wasn't good at – especially sewing – Miss Murphy knew that I liked to sing and was a bit of an actress. She responded to that, and was encouraging when I wasn't playing the goat. I don't think I ever managed to make it clear to Miss Murphy that I liked her, even though she caned me every day.

In 1938 the moneylender told Mam that there was a house to rent in Sackville Street; it had more room and was in better condition than our current house. It was a couple of roads away from Roscommon Street, and the people we called 'the money people' lived there – the midwife, and the man who ran the foundry. I fell in love with the house. It had two pillars outside the entrance door, and decorative stone gateposts with stone baubles on the top. It was the only one like it in the street. I took to it instantly, although if you went into that type of property now, you'd have to spend an awful lot of money renovating it. But in those days private landlords didn't do any repairs or refurbishments; tenants had to do whatever they could for themselves, and for most people that was very little.

The only thing that marred those early months in our

new house was Grandad O'Dowd's death, although like many sad incidents his illness had its funny moments. He'd remarried, and poor Nellie, his second wife, was always the worse for drink – though she was as inoffensive as the day was long. She used to come to Mam, who'd sit her down and give her something to eat.

After Grandad had a stroke, he was taken into hospital. Everyone would be sitting quietly round his bed, and Nellie would come skipping up the ward, having had a few drinks. 'Oooh . . .' Grandad would say, and everyone would laugh. I missed my grandad. I used to take him his dinner every Sunday, and it was strange when he died. It was difficult to get used to not seeing him, but I was going to have to get used to a lot of strange happenings: the war was about to begin.

· 2 ·

The War: A Restless Evacuee

As a thriving port, Liverpool was a natural target during the Second World War. The city was heavily bombed, and many buildings were razed to the ground. Even in the early days of the war, there was a fear of the forthcoming calamities, so many city school-children were evacuated; my younger brother Teddy and I were among them. We were sent to Manor Farm in Church Preen, Shropshire. It was one of the biggest farms in the area, and it was fabulous. For the first time in my life I had my own bedroom, with a highly polished floor, sheepskin rugs, and the most comfortable bed I'd ever slept in. There was everything a child could want. The farmer's wife, Mrs Davies, would stand on a chair and slice bacon from the hams that hung from the kitchen ceiling – she was a lovely cook, and very kind. Her daughter Mary was fourteen, and did her best to try and settle me, but I missed my family and the city streets. It was harvest season, and Mary would take me to their huge orchard to pick apples, Victoria plums and damsons. Mind you, I ate more than I collected. But the Davies weren't concerned about that; they were quite happy for me to eat the fruit if it kept me occupied and prevented me from thinking about home. Nothing could do that for long. I was there only seven days and I cried constantly – I wanted to go home, and I made myself ill with homesickness.

Teddy was all right – he used to go to a little cottage down the lane where they had rabbits and other wildlife. He was only five, and quite happy. But for me it was different: I was ten, and I just couldn't settle. I was a town person in the heart of the country. In the town there was the cinema and all kinds of distractions to excite me. But in the country – oh my goodness! I ran away on more than one occasion – towards Liverpool (as I thought), although I was actually running further away.

Our teachers from school had come with us, and I remember one saying to the other children, 'Take no notice of Frances Barrett if she starts crying; take no notice.' I used to upset all the other poor kids! You can imagine the threatening letters I sent home: what wasn't I going to do if someone didn't come to fetch me!

Then one day, I was walking down the lane and who should I see walking up it but my sister Lizzie. She appeared like an angel. I ran down and grabbed hold of her. We weren't a demonstrative family – we loved each other, but we didn't really show much affection. But I couldn't help myself when I saw our Lizzie walking up the lane in her navy-blue suit.

When we reached the farm she explained to Mrs Davies that she'd come to take me and Teddy home.

Mrs Davies took her round the farmhouse and showed her my room, and everything that was there for me. I must have seemed so ungrateful – she'd put all kinds of things on tap for me, and I didn't appreciate any of them. They were good people, but I wanted to go home, I wanted to be with Mam and Dad (even though I thought he was just a tormentor). I wanted to be home.

While we were still at the farm, our Lizzie threatened me, 'Wait till I tell Mam what a nice place you've stayed at.' I didn't care. Home was where I wanted to be and home was where I was going, come hell or high water. I was a very determined and stubborn child. When we arrived at Lime Street, Lizzie said, 'Go on, you walk first.' I knew why she wanted me to do this – she hadn't got me a ticket.

'Just walk through, it's all right.'

'But you haven't got me a ticket.'

'Bloody walk through that gate, otherwise you'll go back to that farm.' So of course I walked through the gate. I was right: she didn't have a ticket for me, and I didn't like that; I wanted everything to be open and above board – even if I was only ten.

At home there was Mam to face: 'You're a little bitch. Why didn't you stay with that lady? You were on that lovely farm, but you had to cry and say you'd walk home and all that nonsense.'

I hadn't been back long when my older brother Mickey was called up. He must have been about twenty-one or twenty-two, and he was one of the first in our area to be called up. He had to report for duty on the Saturday morning, and collect his uniform.

Mam was out in the back yard cutting up all the cauli-flowers for the cart, and she was crying at the thought of her son going off to war, but she still had to take out the handcart. That night at half-past five she came back because the blackout had started, food was already rationed and there was less to sell. When she got in, Mickey was sitting there in his uniform; he'd been stationed in Seaforth, which was about two minutes' walk from where Mam used to sell the vegetables. She was so relieved.

Mam used to send our Mary and Nellie out every Sunday with Mickey's dinner. They couldn't find Mickey, so they used to sit on the dunes and eat the sandwiches themselves. The cheeky devils would then say to Mam, 'Oh yes, we seen our Mickey, he's doing well, and he enjoyed his dinner.'

Then our Jackie was called up, and all the young lads seemed to disappear into the Army or Navy – some of them never to return. I remember the death of a cousin of mine, Anthony Callaghan. He came home for his twenty-first birthday, and Mam bought a big cake and gave him a party. He went back to his regiment and was killed at Dunkirk. The loss of a young life so early on really hit us. I remember Anthony's curly hair – he was such a handsome lad, and all that life was wasted. I thought at the time that it was a terrible shame; of course I didn't really understand the threat the country was facing.

The radio was the focus of attention in the war years – we'd sit by it, listening to the news and hearing about the ships that had been sunk in the Atlantic. People were devastated. The majority of seamen were from the

Merseyside area; everyone had someone either going away to sea or working on the docks. Those were the main industries of the region. I'll never forget Mam and Dad standing to attention, listening to the wireless, and seeing their faces so full of concern.

At school we used to have siren drills in preparation for air raids. On one occasion, we all filed out and the girls had to sit on the staircase. Sister Phillip wanted someone to entertain the pupils. Guess who put her hand up?

'Frances Barrett, come on then, you sing for us.'

So I got up and started: 'Ma, he's making eyes at me . . .' I sang about three lines before I saw Sister looking at me with utter and absolute contempt. She held a little piece of the shoulder of my dress between her thumb and finger, as if she didn't want to be contaminated by me, and guided me right back to my place on the stair. 'Sit down!' I was so deflated. I felt terrible, but I didn't realise that it was the type of song I was singing that so offended her. It was hardly the wisest choice of song for a ten-year-old in a Catholic school. The next girl she called upon to sing was Mary Rigby, from a really staunch Catholic family, and I remember her song to this day: 'It's no universe, and I've got the time to spare, I've got a pocket full of dreams . . .' That was acceptable. There was nothing suggestive or naughty about that, so Sister smiled at Mary, and continued to give me the daggers!

When the bombing intensified, the school closed and it was decided that we would be taught in people's houses. This didn't work very well as lots of children didn't bother to attend, but those of us who did thought it was absolutely fantastic. We'd be there for only about an hour, then we'd be sent home. Consequently, our education was seriously affected by the war. I'm not saying that I would have won a scholarship, but the opportunity was never there, because of the hostilities. There again, some of the children from families that were more acceptable to the Catholic hierarchy received some private tuition from the teachers and headmistress.

In the spring of 1940 my niece Kathleen came to live with us. Our Lizzie had a new baby, and Mam said, 'Oh, poor Lizzie's not going to be able to look after three children with only three years between them. We'll take Kathleen until she gets on her feet.' I took Kathleen to see Lizzie a couple of times a week, and they said, 'All right, Kathleen, you can stay here with your mother now,' but she always wanted to come home with me. I used to tease her. I'd hide, and she'd be crying her eyes out; real cruel it was. She wouldn't let me go. I had no intention of leaving her, but she didn't know that and would follow me everywhere.

Once Kathleen knocked over a kettle, pouring boiling water from her elbow to her wrist. I used to take her to the hospital because she wouldn't go with anyone else. She started screaming when they took the bandages off her arm. She sat on my knee, and I was crying and she was crying. The nurse said to me, 'I don't know what you're crying for, dear. There's nothing wrong with you.' But I was crying because our poor Kathleen was in such pain.

On the radio, Liverpool was never specifically mentioned for being bombed; you heard only of 'the northwest'. This was a propaganda exercise because Liverpool was a strategic target for enemy bombers, but it demoralised the people of the city because they felt – as they feel today for different reasons – that they were ignored and perceived to be of no consequence. The most appalling time was the Christmas blitz of 1940, when Liverpool was bombed night after night. One evening, the bombs were raining down, and at about seven o'clock we heard a terrible noise. No one knew what it was. We were all cowering in a cubbyhole in the cellar, and everyone was reciting their rosary. I don't think Our Lord had ever heard as many prayers as he did that night as we mumbled to him in our fear.

At midnight a rat-tat-tat came at the door, over and over again. My dad said, 'I'll open that door.' He'd never in his life been known to volunteer to take a kettle off the stove – even if he was sitting next to it – let alone open a door. Everyone else had to do it for him. But he insisted: 'I'll open this door, it could be parachutists.' Well, we were really impressed by his bravery when we imagined German parachutists at the door.

When he got upstairs, he put on his strongest voice: 'Who's that at that door?'

'It's the police. Open up.'

The noise had been caused by a bomb that had dropped in the street, but hadn't exploded. 'Everyone out. Don't take anything, just *get out*. It's liable to go off at any minute.'

Everyone panicked. Our Mary said to Teddy, who was five at the time, 'Jump on me back,' so that she could carry him up the stairs. But when she got up the stairs, she found out that it was Jackie who'd jumped on her back, and he was fifteen! Such was the confusion we were all in.

Somehow we got to the door, and in the dark street everyone split up. Our Nellie, Mam and Teddy went one way; Katherine, Mary, Jackie and I went another. You've got to bear in mind that bombs were still dropping, there were fires everywhere, and the noise and swooshing of explosions. To a child, it was terrifying.

We were herded into China Street, with its large Salvation Army building. Everyone from the area was there, while fires raged on the dock and all over Liverpool. The Salvation Army women and men looked after us, coming round with hot tea and cocoa, hot milk for the children, and biscuits. Someone started to play the organ, to raise people's spirits, and the men were asked if they had to go to work, and at what time, so that they could get some sleep at a different end of the hall. If you didn't go to work during the war, without a valid reason, you were jailed or fined.

This happened on a Friday night, a week before Christmas. I'd run out the house with no shoes or stockings on; all I was wearing my knickers, vest and a gymslip – no coat, no cardigan, no jumper. But I don't remember feeling the cold.

My mam went to my auntie's and stayed the night there. When she arrived on Saturday morning I said, 'I'm not staying here. I'm going off to our Lizzie's with Kathleen and Teddy.'

That night, the raids started again. Mill Road maternity hospital was bombed, and all the babies and a lot of the women died. Lizzie's house was only about forty yards away. I sat crying on the settee and saying my prayers, with Lizzie and Billy laughing at my fervour and saying, 'It'll be all right, Franny,' trying to calm me down.

The next morning I walked around Mill Road. All I could see was rubble and the debris was still smoking and smouldering, while a terrible smell hung in the air. I went back to Lizzie's and said, 'I'm not staying here either.' She wouldn't let me take Kathleen, so Teddy and I went to Auntie Sarah's in Huyton, seven or eight miles away. The days rolled on towards Christmas, and we were there for Christmas Day itself. We hung up our stockings and Margaret, my cousin, put a few three-penny bits in their toes and filled them up with cinders. Of course we grieved for Mam, Dad and the rest of the family, but at least we were safe, and it was such a relief to go to bed without being frightened of the bombs.

The blitz ended during the Christmas period. We went back home, but it was thought too dangerous for us to stay in the city, so we children were sent away again. The second evacuation began on 11 February 1941. I remember Teddy and I getting on the train. This time I was determined: 'I'm not going to cry. Others have to go away, and I'll try my best. Soldiers and sailors have to go away; I'll have to be the same and be as brave as I can.' It was like a resolution.

We travelled from Lime Street Station to Aberystwyth, and our teachers spent the journey filling in forms about our background and welfare, saying she or he needs this or that. The teacher didn't ask me one of the questions, but I saw him write down the answer. Under 'Circumstances' he wrote 'Poor'. This was a real shock to me; I'd never realised till that day that we were classed as poor. I thought we had a pretty decent life, and I'd never considered myself as deprived: whatever I wanted, I got.

At Aberystwyth we piled on to buses, and drove for two or three hours to Cardigan. When we arrived we were brought into the county school hall, sat down and given Irish stew. I think everyone knew that Liverpool people ate scouse, and this was the nearest way to make us feel at home. It was a nice gesture, although I've never been keen on scouse and would always pull a face when my mam put a plate of it in front of me. There were 150 children from five different parishes in Liverpool.

By the time we'd been examined by the doctor we were all a bit bewildered and tired. I was just twelve and Teddy was seven, and I'd said I'd keep an eye on a young boy called Tucker Bore. A number of people came and asked if I would like to go and live with them, but I refused: 'No, thank you.' There was one woman who reminded me of a music-hall or radio character called Mrs Feather who wore funny little hats. She had a hotel, but I didn't want to go and live with a Mrs Feather.

Then Auntie came up. She had a gentle, homely manner, and when she asked, 'Would you like to come and stay with me?' I said, 'Yes, I would, and can I bring me brother?' and she said, 'Yes.' Then I said, 'Can I bring Tucker?' When she said 'Yes' again, we were all quite happy.

Auntie lived in Ebens Lane, off the High Street. The house was only tiny – but oh, it had such a lovely atmosphere, so cosy and welcoming! The three of us slept together in one bed, and we loved it there. However, we didn't always see eye to eye with Auntie's son, Dave. He was only five years old and as an only child, he was used to getting his own way. When he was naughty, Auntie would threaten him by saying, 'Dave, I'm going to count up to five and if you haven't stopped playing about by then, there'll be trouble.' I used to silently will Dave to carry on acting the goat so that he'd get a slap, but Auntie counted *so* slowly that he always got away with it – to my utter disgust. Despite Auntie's soft treatment of her son, we idolised her, and if there is a heaven, Auntie's going to be there, and Uncle Eric too.

After about three months she found the strain of coping with three boys too great, so Teddy and Tucker were given new placements. Teddy went to Mr and Mrs Evans and their two unmarried daughters, who absolutely idolised him. If I went to ask if I could take Teddy to the pictures or wherever, they'd be there to meet him, standing outside the cinema with their stout walking sticks. They'd call him: 'C'mon, Ted,' and he'd get really embarrassed, because Teddy was a man's man: he didn't want to be messing around with girls, and would rather be with Mr Evans hearing about when he worked on the ships in Liverpool. Tucker was sent – you might think I'm making this up, but I'm not – to live with the lady who I'd thought was

Mrs Feather. He went to the White Hart Hotel, and was really happy there.

I stayed with Auntie, and Tucker's sister, Minto (Mary) came down; Auntie said that she could stay as well. She and I got on fine together, although I think she was only about six. Uncle Eric's sister, Sybil, also stayed with us. She was a bit of a snob and insisted that we call her Miss Street, but she wasn't bad.

Auntie didn't cook an evening meal. She said apologetically, 'You can go to the chip shop at the top of the street and get fish and chips from there.' That was like heaven to me, going to the chippy at the end of the road, yet she was more or less making out that this was deprivation. We loved it!

We often had singsongs. Auntie had a piano in the parlour, and Uncle had a set of drums. We'd sing 'Somewhere over the Rainbow' and all the other favourites. Uncle Eric used to get all sorts of music sent to him from London; he'd get music that hardly anyone had heard of. They used to sing Max Miller's 'Meet Me in the Blackout, Sweetheart', and I'd join in as well: 'Meet me in the blackout, sweetheart, With your gas mask on your arm/I don't care . . .' Auntie would allow my friends, whoever called for me, to come in and play the drums and the piano if they wished. It was more or less an open-house invitation. She was fantastic, that woman.

Sometimes I did get homesick. I remember listening to 'Hi Gang' or 'Sailors Ahoy' and starting to cry, and Uncle Eric saying, 'Sailors don't cry. Oh Fran, you're really good, you've been very brave. Sailors don't cry.' That brought me round.

We went to the national school in Cardigan. One part of the building was reserved for the evacuees, the other part for the Welsh children. After a week or two there was a natural rivalry between us and the Welshees, and we were going to give them what-for. There were a few skirmishes, but on the whole we mixed well.

Cardigan was a lovely place. We walked for miles to the beach at Gwbert, to swim. There were very strong tidal currents, but we didn't realise this until one girl, Teresa Cushion, was swept out to sea. Her name was appropriate, because she had the presence of mind to float on her back, and she was scooped up by some Cardigan fishermen. After that we were forbidden to go to the beach unless we had a teacher with us.

One of my favourite teachers, Miss O'Shaunessy, had accompanied us and we all got on fine with her, but she had to go home for some reason. We were all upset and wondered who would replace her. When the day came, we stood at the bus stop awaiting the new arrival with some trepidation. As the teachers were responsible for our well-being, they had quite a large role in our lives as evacuees. Who should walk off the bus but – yes, you've guessed it: Miss Murphy! I am absolutely sure she gave a groan when she saw me. She must have thought: Oh no, here we go again. But when she knew that I was settled, she was great.

There was one thing, however, all we girls were annoyed by. We were twelve or thirteen – and we all thought the world of a young Welshman, who must have been about twenty. Roy Daniel was fabulous to look at. We'd all talk about him, and we'd shout, 'Hi

Roy', as soon as we saw him, and run across the street and make a fuss of him. But then along came Miss Murphy. She'd only been there a few months and next thing, she was courting Roy. When she started courting, none of us was allowed to call him Roy any more; we had to call him Mr Daniel! We thought that was a bit of a cheek, when we knew him first!

On the Guildhall steps, in the High Street, was a cannon which supposedly dated from the Crimean War. It was a natural meeting-place and we all used to sit on the gun, jump over the wheels and generally make a nuisance of ourselves, having a giggle and a laugh. This was right in the centre of the small town, and we didn't realise that we were in everyone's eye-view.

My friend Jean lived with one of the doctors, whose wife was very annoyed with her for playing on the cannon because it wasn't the done thing. She said to me, 'Frances, do *you* play on the cannon?' Of course I told her a barefaced lie: 'Oh no, Mrs Lloyd Davies.'

'Oh,' she said, 'Jean does. Would you like to come and live with me?'

My butter-wouldn't-melt answer had put me on the spot. I didn't want to live with her; I was happy where I was with Auntie. I didn't want to try and be the big I-am, but I thought I should tell Auntie about our conversation. She was a little upset and said that I could go to stay with Mrs Lloyd Davies if I wanted to, but she knew I didn't.

I was in Cardigan for about ten months. During the summer a telegram arrived to say that my mother was coming down to see us. Teddy and I were overjoyed and went to the station to meet her. There was no nicer sight than Mam getting off that train and, God help her, she'd been travelling from about eight o'clock in the morning and it was about nine at night. We took her home, and she'd brought all sorts of little gifts for Auntie. She was very grateful to her for taking me and Teddy in, giving us good food, clothing, a lovely bed to sleep in, and generally looking after us. My mam was full of humility to the lady.

There wasn't much to see in Cardigan – there was just the main street and a few little streets off it – but we took her all round. I think she was with us for only about three or four days, and then she had to go home. Auntie knew that we were upset, so she took us out to see her mother, who lived on a farm. She spoke only Welsh, but she always managed to make us laugh and used to show me how to pat butter in the dairy with little wooden paddles. But there was more sadness to come, and this was another reason that Auntie had taken us to the farm as a distraction.

Auntie said, 'Frances, come with me. Auntie Jane wants some blackberries to make an apple and blackberry pie. Come out and we'll pick them.' It's funny the way things stick out in your memory.

'Frances,' she said, 'I've got something to tell you, and I know you'll be upset. But you need to know.' And she told me about Lizzie's Kathleen. Kathleen had died of meningitis, with the raids and everything. There wasn't an awful lot that the medical profession could do about meningitis in those days; very few people survived it. Kathleen was only three. I was so upset by the news, and I was also upset because I wasn't there to see her, or to mourn for her with Lizzie and Mam and all the family. Poor little Kathleen – she was such a lovely child. Auntie told me about Kathleen while we picked the blackberries, and she put her arms around me, comforting me, as we stood in the kitchen garden.

Soon afterwards, I received my first ever present from a boy. I never thought I was very attractive – I never gave myself any credit really, when I should have done; I didn't have the confidence. We'd made friends with the Welsh children. There was one boy in particular called Richard – no, not Richard Burton, Richard Jenkins. One evening we were all sitting on the cannon and I said, 'I'll have to go, I've got to be in for eight o'clock.'

Richard said, 'Frances, I've bought these for you.' He gave me a quarter-pound box of Dairy Milk chocolates.

I was so shaken, I didn't know what to say. All I managed was 'Oh, thanks very much, Richard. Good night.'

That was it. I just went home. But it was an exciting event for me. Of course we all thought of boys, we all had our pet lads whom we liked (quite apart from Roy Daniel, who was beyond our reach). I liked Aiden White, but he wouldn't look at anyone . . .

Mr Merryman was in charge of us at school. We called him Merrylegs because he had the habit of standing in front of the class with one hand behind his back and the other pinching his moustache, and at the same time he would bend his knees like a caricature of a policeman. He was very strict, and stood no nonsense. Looking back, I suppose that he had a great responsibility, and he had to keep control of us.

On one occasion, servicemen stationed in a nearby town heard that Cardigan housed evacuees from Liverpool, and, as many of them were also from Liverpool, they decided to give us a day out. These young servicemen, who received only a pittance, raised enough money to take all us children to Aberporth and provided cakes, sweets (which were rationed), games and races, and made a really memorable day for us. Those who won a race were presented with a prize, and I was given a tennis ball. I think my expression must have mirrored my disappointment, because Mr Merryman sent for me and said, 'Frances, didn't you like your prize?' I didn't want to seem ungrateful, so I said, 'Yes, Sir', but he knew I didn't, and allowed me to exchange it for a girls' storybook.

Another incident was more in keeping with his reputation. A group of girls and boys went to the local shop, 'Peacocks', which was the nearest thing to Woolworth's in the town, and temptation being what it is, someone took a pair of socks. They were all rounded up and taken to Mr Merryman, who laid into them for bringing disgrace on us all. As it happens, I was not with the crowd that day, so I was looked on as a goody-goody which didn't sit too well on my shoulders, but at least that day I escaped the teacher's wrath.

Mr Nicholls was totally different from Mr Merryman – he was very jovial, and took it upon himself to be a peacemaker if any evacuee found themselves in trouble. Auntie's crockery was of very good quality and once, when I was putting dishes back on the Welsh dresser, when one of the plates tipped against another and the whole lot came crashing down. I looked at Auntie in dismay, and I could see that she was extremely annoyed with me. I said how sorry I was, and that I would save up and buy her some new ones (although how I was going to do that I don't know). I went out of the house feeling really upset at my clumsiness, and bumped into Mr Nicholls. I started to weep, but he took hold of my hand and tried to assure me that everything would be all right. That caused another dilemma, because I thought Auntie would think I was frightened of her if Mr Nicholls went to plead on my behalf. He was very diplomatic, however, and everything was sorted out. Auntie put her arms around me and said, 'It's all right, Frances, we'll forget all about it.' Fortunately, that episode ended well. Mr Nicholls was always there for the children who were in his charge.

We were in Cardigan until the autumn. The bombing had stopped in Liverpool, and I said that I was going home. I wanted to be home for Christmas. My mam said it was all right, so Teddy and I got our cases packed up. Auntie was crying and I was crying; Uncle Eric was crying and Minto was crying. We got on the bus with Mr Merryman and Miss Murphy, and Teddy and I went on to Liverpool's Central Station. I remember my dad being there to meet us. As ever, he didn't hug us or anything, he just said 'Ello'. Teddy had a great big box, and as my dad wasn't a robust man in his later years, he couldn't carry it up the stairs. The porter lifted it without any effort, and led us to a taxi. It was the first time I'd ever been in one.

Being home was another kind of a shock. We were really delighted to be there, but we'd been living in an entirely different environment, and now we had to revert back to where we'd lived before. Everything seemed strange, and it took me a while to readjust.

Our school had been bombed while I was away, and all the girls had to squeeze downstairs in the infants. There were about fifty of us in the class. Some afternoons we'd have some boring subjects, and to get out of those and absorb some time, I'd put my hand up and say, 'Sister, did you know that there's been an advance at Tobruk?' Being a nun, Sister never listened to the radio. All the information she could glean came from either the children or the teachers. I'd go into the whole account about the offensive in the Middle East, and how the morale of the soldiers had to be kept up, etc., and after about half an hour she'd say, 'If it wasn't for Frances, I wouldn't know what's going on in this war.' I don't think she realised my motive for educating her on the subject. She was a good teacher and taught us how to appreciate Dickens and Robert Burns, and as she was a Scot, we knew all the Scottish songs and history. She was progressive, and taught us things that she knew would come in handy in later years. For me, they did. I never expected, when I was making them giggle at school, that I would be dining in the homes of high sheriffs in the years to come.

· 3 ·

Laughter and Sorrows

In April 1943 I left school and started work at Littlewoods Pools, the major employer of women in Liverpool. I was just fourteen: a schoolgirl on Friday afternoon and a wage-earner on Monday morning. I was full of apprehension, but there were lots of young girls in the same boat. I was put into the primary sorting room, where we had to fold and file the envelopes in alphabetical order before they were sent on to another depot for further categorisation. Unlike today, Littlewoods didn't provide envelopes, and because of the war everything had to be reused. We'd be sifting through envelopes that had been back and forth three or four times, getting shabbier with each journey. Because of my sense of humour I soon found that I could entertain everyone, and I'd have all the other girls laughing. Of course my work suffered. I remember one of the supervisors saying emphatically to me, 'Miss Barrett, do you think that this is the right job for you?' 'Oh yes,' I replied, with a polite smile.

My stay in Littlewoods was very happy, although during this time I reached adolescence. I think all teenagers are a bit self-conscious, and I was no exception. I was only five foot four and a half, and by the age of fifteen or sixteen I weighed about ten stone. That didn't sit well on me. Moreover, it wasn't really the done thing to have a big bust; it wasn't fashionable, and unfortunately I was out of fashion. I didn't think my nose was very nice, or my hair; in fact I was displeased with the whole lot. Some of the girls used to come into work looking beautiful, but I felt that the only thing I had going for me was my stature. My father had always made us walk straight, and sit up without slouching. I think that stood me in good stead, and I was able to carry off the clothes I wore. Mind you, clothes were rationed and restricted.

You were issued with twenty-four coupons to last twelve months; if a man needed a suit it cost twenty-six coupons, and if he didn't want to wait for his next allocation he had to resort to the black market, where you could buy a coupon for a shilling. That was a lot of money in those days. As I was only on my first wage – 12s. 6d. – the black market was beyond my means, but I had a keen eye for a good deal, and the second-hand markets were my territory. If you wanted a coat, however, you went to the shops in town. To save material, all coats were standard length – just below the knee – and no one could have anything longer (or shorter, for that matter) unless they cut it themselves. If you bought a coat with a half lining, it cost seven or eight coupons; without any lining at all it was about six. Although you saved by sparing the lining, the coarse material rubbed your arms and the back of your neck.

As a result, people were pretty inventive. The mother

of my friend Eileen could do anything with a sewing machine. If you had an old coat, Mrs Lawler would unpick it and measure it out for a pinafore dress; she'd also show you how to do the same. I used to say, 'I couldn't possibly do that, Mrs Lawler,' and she'd say, 'Oh yes you can. Come on, I'll show you.' That was the type of woman she was: she didn't keep her trade secrets to herself. She kept an eye out for materials on sale, and she could make dresses for me and Eileen out of practically nothing. She once made us dance dresses from a large piece of black velvet; they had short puffed sleeves and heart-shaped necklines. The only problem was that the velvet clung to the inside of my coat, and by the time I got to the dance the dress was around my neck!

Dance dresses were the glamorous side of wartime, so it was hardly surprising that material was hard to come by, but even the most basic things were in short supply. With the blackout, the streets were incredibly dark, especially during the winter, yet you couldn't get hold of a torch for love or money. They'd be the talk of the neighbourhood – 'Hey, what's-his-name has got a smashing torch; have you seen it?' You wouldn't think anything so mundane would be the highlight of conversation, but it was. Sausages were difficult to find as well, and the word would go round when a butcher had a supply of them. We seemed to spend half the war standing in queues outside the butcher's shop. We were allowed only one shilling and twopence worth of meat; that would buy perhaps half a pound of steak to last the week, so we had to be very careful with our rations.

When my brothers came home on leave, we were

issued with an emergency ration card. My dad used to say to me, 'You go down to Brabins.' They were the main meat importers in Liverpool, and had a shop in the city centre. The man there got to know me because I was a little bit cheeky. I'd go down to the shop with three ration cards: one for Billy Pringle (my brother-in-law), one for our Jackie, and one for our Mickey. It was always a great occasion when all the lads were home at the same time, and my mam provided the best meal for them that she could.

When the butcher asked, 'What do you want, girl?' I said, 'Can I have a leg of lamb?' The man nearly collapsed on the floor laughing, and he shouted into the back, 'Hey, Joe, d'you know that little kid that comes here? She only wants a leg of lamb.' I must have got about five bob's worth of rations; they always gave me more than I was due because I was so forthright.

Of course fruit and vegetables were also scarce, and it was lucky that Mam sold them, but as a teenager I was a bit ashamed that she went out with a handcart. I shouldn't have been; she was a hardworking woman and very lovable, but at that age I wanted her to be a shopkeeper. In order to impress a girl who worked with me at Littlewoods I told her that Mam had a fruit shop and the news somehow spread. It was the time of the potato shortage, when potatoes were strictly allocated. This girl said to me, 'Do you think your mother would let me have five pounds of potatoes?' I didn't even have the bottle to say, 'No, sorry, they're for her customers.' I was trying to be the big one, so I said, 'Yes, I'll get them for you – no problem.'

Once I'd committed myself, I had to do it. I'd bring

the potatoes to this girl and she'd be really grateful. She paid me, but I couldn't give my mother the money because then she'd know I'd been at the potato sack. When I look back now, I think: Oh God, why did I do that? But it was funny at the time.

Despite all the scrimping and the juggling of rations, we had a lot of laughs. My sisters Lizzie and Nellie worked in the Royal Ordinance Factory, making munitions, and as war workers they received some concessions. I was a great cinema fan – I practically lived in the 4d. seats of the stalls – and sometimes they could get cheap tickets. One Saturday our Lizzie gave me her ticket to go and see *Gone With the Wind*. As usual, Mam had gone out with the handcart, and it was my job to fetch the rations, but our Mary said I could go to the pictures as long as I finished the errands. I raced around and did all the shopping, but in my haste I forgot the salt fish. Salt fish was a Sunday morning ritual, and woe betide me if I came home without it. There wasn't time to go back for it and still catch the start of the film, but I promised Mary that I'd collect it from town.

I jumped on a tramcar that took me to the cinema and a long queue of about forty or fifty yards long, and four deep. Everyone was panicking in case they didn't get in. I asked a woman to save my place while I hotfooted it to the fishmonger's. It hardly seems credible, but I sat through three hours of *Gone With the Wind* with the salt fish on my knee. At the end of the film there were two empty seats on either side of me – not so much 'gone with the wind' as downwind!

I went to the pictures on my first date. I think the lad

was only about seventeen, and I was fifteen. His name was Bobby Curry, and I think he was in the Army. He lived in Garibaldi Street. Bobby asked me to go out, and oh, first date – gosh! After the film, he brought me home to the door and said, 'Good night. I'll see you tomorrow.' I said, 'All right,' but on the following night he called for me at the house, and Dad just said, 'You've come here for my daughter? She's only fifteen. You go and hop it!' And the poor lad had to go!

The highlight of our days was when one of the lads came home. You'd open the door to see them standing there in their good uniform with their buttons polished, carrying everything they owned – rifle, tin hat, haversack, kit bag – the lot. They were like gods to us. Being young, we didn't realise the dangers they'd been in, and how lonely and frightening war is. They brought cigarettes and sweets – all sorts of things – and we were simply delighted. When someone came home – it didn't have to be a member of our family – everyone in the neighbourhood got together, and they'd say, 'Whose house is having the do tonight?' Everyone would congregate for the party, especially if the manager of the pub agreed to have his allocation of Guinness in; there'd be queues a mile long for Guinness.

One night, when there'd been a raid on, there was a knock at the door, and my dad went to open it. I'll give my dad his due: for all his faults and failings, he always opened the door during the war. 'Who is it?' he said, and a voice called out: 'It's Billy Seddon.' Mr Seddon lived next door. He said, 'You've got a visitor – it's Catherine's brother.'

It was Willie, Mam's brother who'd been sent to Canada. Willie had joined the Army, and been sent to England. Now that he was on leave, he'd tracked Mam down, and he'd brought a friend with him. He came into the house, and everyone started crying and laughing. My mam was saying, 'Oh, our poor Willie,' over and over again. She hadn't seen him for – I think – twenty-eight years.

The lad with him was a bit bewildered. His name was Paul, and he couldn't speak English – he was a French Canadian. Willie spoke fluent French, but he was the spitting image of my mam; they were like two peas in a pod. Everyone was delighted. He'd brought bars of chocolate, tins of fruit – everything. All the family came round to see Uncle Willie, and there were parties galore. He came home on leave a few times after that, and each time he brought somebody with him. He had the same trait as my mam; she was like that. If you were a friend of hers, you were a friend of the whole family.

Willie was as good as gold – until he'd had a drink. Oh, then he was crackers. He used to let the drink take hold of him, and it was like the Jekyll and Hyde syndrome. Uncle Willie really used to carry on a bit. My dad didn't say anything about it. Normally, he'd have said, 'Hey, off you pop,' before you could blink an eye, but he didn't, because me mam hadn't seen her brother for such a long time. Eventually there was a big row, and Willie left because of it. After that I think he wrote to my Mam a few times, but we never saw him again.

1945 was an exciting year. Everyone knew that Germany had been defeated, and that it was only a matter of time before the war was over; anticipation filled the air. When the time came, the boss walked into our room at Littlewoods and said, 'You've got the rest of the day off.' We all went home, but there was no official announcement that night. I went to bed, and all of a sudden the bells started to ring. Thinking of it now, I could cry. We hadn't heard the bells since 1939, because they had been the signal for an invasion. The bells pealed all over Liverpool. People got up from their beds, shoved anything on, and went outside. We walked from Sackville Street to St George's Hall, Lime Street. It was about two o'clock in the morning, and an amazing sight: thousands and thousands of people, all happy, all singing, and most of them crying with joy. Some were crying because they'd lost loved ones, but the sense of euphoria was electric.

The next day, the 8th of May, nobody went to work. Everyone went into the city centre. There were people with piano-key boxes, banjos, guitars, drums, and I remember some girls dressed in Hawaiian costumes dancing on the steps of St George's Hall. Mam and her friends got out the handcart and took it in turns to push one another down to Lime Street. Me mam, who was built like a little tank, ended up sitting on one of the lions down there. They were all absolutely over the moon. It was such a memorable occasion.

Once the excitement was over, we had to get back to work. The war with Japan was still on, and it was August before Japan surrendered, with the horrific bombing of Hiroshima and Nagasaki. Of course people didn't understand the consequences of those bombings. We learned only of our prisoners of war, their skin taut over their faces and bodies just like skeletons. And of those horrific scenes that were described, of all the poor people, degraded, dehumanised, abused and murdered in Belsen. Robbie Burns said, 'Man's inhumanity to man makes countless thousands mourn,' and countless thousands did mourn those mounds of bones, and the shock and horror on the faces of the Allied soldiers and the MPs who went to see what had happened in Germany. Oh my God, when we heard we just cried.

The rest of that year was something of an anticlimax, although it was a brilliant piece of work when a Labour government was returned at the general election. Whoever would believe now that before the Labour victory there were no paid holidays, you couldn't go to the doctor without paying threepence, or joining a penny-in-the-pound club so that you could pay your prescription, and you couldn't order an ambulance without having to pay?

The Labour government gave new hope for the country and for the working class in particular, but our anticipation of a new deal was blighted by tragedy. Our Lizzie had taken ill in 1941. Dr Briery gave her notes so that she could stay off work without the risk of being fined, but he didn't examine her. We thought she had a heavy cough or a chill, but in fact she had a shadow on her lung. During the war we'd moved from Number 29 Sackville Street to Number 10, crossing over the road. It's said to be fatal to cross to a house on the opposite side of the road; according to legend, your luck changes. Ours certainly did. Lizzie's condition deteriorated, and she was sent to Heswell Sanatorium. Her two daughters, Marie and May, stayed with us while her husband Billy was away at the war. On Wednesdays and Sundays we used to go and visit her. You were allowed to visit only twice a week, but Mam used to sneak in on Tuesdays because the nurses got to know her. With the dedication of a mother, she'd walk nearly five miles to see Lizzie, and take her whatever she wanted.

Sometimes Lizzie was allowed to come home for weekends, and during 1945 she came home for some months. She had a bed in the parlour – that was her domain. Although she was ill, she wasn't demoralised. Lizzie had a happy disposition and everyone enjoyed visiting her, despite our misery at seeing her failing health.

In the spring of the following year, with Lizzie at home, I set off for work a bit late one morning. My dad hadn't called me as he usually did, but he'd been feeling a bit off colour. I'd made arrangements to go with my friend Maggie to the Shakespeare theatre that evening (we used to go at least twice a week). After work, as I came into the back yard and went up the steps, my friend Eileen's mother, Mrs Lawler, was standing there. I could see that she was upset, but when I asked, 'What's the matter?' she simply shook her head in silence.

I dashed into the house and our Marie said, 'Franny, Grandad's dead.'

'You're a naughty girl,' I said, 'saying things like that.'

Then everyone started crying. My Dad had died in his sleep. He was fifty-six, he'd been ill only a couple of days. The shock was terrible, it shook us to our roots. That was 1 March 1946.

On the same day our Catherine, my eldest sister, was taken into hospital and gave birth to a little boy, Michael. Three days later Michael died. Catherine didn't know about Dad because she was too ill herself, so we brought the baby home, and Michael was buried with him. On the day of the funeral our Mickey came home on compassionate leave, but he arrived too late for the service, which was awful for him. Two deaths within three days: that was the start of our tragedies.

Our Lizzie stayed at home, but she started to deteriorate rapidly. Billy was demobbed, so he was able to look after Lizzie, and he was very good to her. She had Communion practically every day. Father Doyle came to the house, and he would bring nourishing titbits for her, but Lizzie's decline continued. She went into hospital once more, and died there on 22 September.

I can't put into words the devastation we felt during that time. It was torturous. My dad's death had been so unexpected, I couldn't control my grief. He was a funny creature, a very strict man who idolised his family and was extremely protective of us, even though he couldn't show his emotions – you knew you were in his good books only if he called you 'Daughter'. His death was shattering; we didn't think anything could hit us as hard as that, but then came baby Michael's tragically short life and the numbing pain of Lizzie's death. It was unbelievable that all this could happen within six months.

· 4 ·

Marriage and Tenement Life

The following year I decided to join the Land Army –
I was feeling restless, and I wanted a break from the
painful memories at home. I was called up straight
away and sent to a farm just outside Bedford, where I
was billeted in a mansion house with twenty other girls.
I quickly discovered that I wasn't cut out for farming.
I was terrified of the cows, and wouldn't go near the
horses. Nor did I take to working in the fields. We were
out potato-picking until we thought our backs would
break, and in the evenings our appetite was ferocious;
we'd eat everything and anything that was put before
us. And oh, I was homesick; I wanted to go back to
Liverpool.

After three weeks I had my first weekend leave,
which turned out to be my last. When I described the
work to Mrs Gannon, the mother of my friend Maggie,
her response was plain: 'Don't you go back there,
Franny, your father would go mad if he knew; you stay
at home.' I never went back, and Mrs Gannon even
returned my uniform for me to spare me from having
to explain myself. My great adventure came to a swift

end, but of course I was now unemployed and had to sign on the dole.

Fortunately, I wasn't out of work for long; I was taken on as an addressograph operator for Liverpool Corporation. I used to print all the electricity bills. The money wasn't as good as it had been at Littlewoods, but I was glad to be working from nine till five again, and I liked the job. There were about eight of us in a little office, and I used to sing to entertain everyone; I'd sing little snippets of opera – not that I knew opera, but I'd heard pieces on the radio. The women would often say, 'Oh, Frances, go and get your voice trained.' We also harmonised and sang the Andrews Sisters' 'Rum and Coca-Cola' as we worked.

Now that I was earning a wage once more, I fell back into the old routine of going to all the dances. I was fanatical. Every Sunday Maggie Gannon and I would attend the All Souls' church dance for one and six. It was still difficult to get clothes because of rationing, and it was often a case of make do and mend. We drooled over the stylish dresses that actresses wore in films like *State Fair*, and did our best with what we had; in the summer we went to the dance with roses in our hair, and thought we were the height of sophistication. Sometimes Maggie's uncle, who was often overseas, brought back dresses for her – they were heavenly, well cut and well made, and quite different from what we could buy in Liverpool. I drooled over them.

By this stage I'd lost my puppy fat and had a nice figure and good legs, which really boosted my confidence. We'd go to the church hall and stand chatting in a group, trying not to look as if we were waiting to be asked to dance, although of course we were. But I had one dress that always brought me success. My mam had found it at the second-hand market – it was maroon, with a flared skirt. It fitted me to a T, and I was just like Moira Shearer in *The Red Shoes* – whenever I wore that magical dress, I never sat down: all the lads asked me to dance.

It was at one of the dances that I met Michael (Mick) Clarke, who was to become my husband. He asked to take me home, and as I thought he was a nice lad, I said 'All right'. He took me home a few times, then we started to go out with each other. On our first date we went to see a film called *Deception*. When we went into the cinema, I sat down and took out my glasses. Mick has always said that he never got over the shock of seeing me put those glasses on! 'I'm not going to sit here and not see the film,' I thought (though it was dreadful, and I wouldn't have missed much). The next day we went to see *Romance at Rosy Ridge*, and followed it with *I Wonder Who's Kissing Her Now*.

That was the beginning of our courtship, just after my nineteenth birthday. Mick would meet me from work and we'd go for walks. We really enjoyed each other's company; he was very humorous, and could always see jokes where the casual observer might not. He was also very generous and a hard worker. He was only seventeen, and he was a carter, which was really heavy work. He used to feed the horses at five o'clock in the morning every day of the week, clean out the stables and put down new straw. There wasn't an awful lot of money in the job, and he was out in all weathers.

Michael liked the animals, but it wasn't a job with any prospects, so he went to work in a timber yard with his brother Patrick, whom we called Patsy.

Patsy also had a girlfriend, and he encouraged Mick to bring me home to tea so that my visit would break the ice, then he could follow suit. So, with some apprehension, I was presented at the doorstep for Sunday tea. I needn't have been nervous – the family took me into the parlour and made me very welcome. They had a fabulous Ekco radiogram – that was really something in 1948 – and stacks and stacks of records, which were very well looked after.

Those records became a ritual. Mick's favourite singer was Jimmy Rogers, but I preferred Danny Kaye with his 'Bleep Bloop' and 'Deana', and I loved Bing Crosby, and Grandad Clarke would sing 'Love in Bloom' whenever we came into the house. Mick's older brother, Bernie, was completely different; he loved Wagner. 'Just listen to this,' he used to say to me, and I would have to admit that the music was really melodious. Bernie always used to say that I was his Brünhilde from *Tristan and Isolde*, though I can't imagine myself coming over the hill with a pair of horns on my head and long blonde hair. He really was a dedicated fan, yet working-class families weren't encouraged to have any knowledge of classical music.

It was a happy household, and I spent a lot of time there. I was very outgoing, whereas Mick was reticent; he had a quietening influence on me – or at least he tried. I don't think he succeeded, but we made a good couple, and at the end of the year we decided to get married.

The wedding took place on 27 December 1948. It was a funny event. We only had one wedding car, and I think it took about four journeys to get us to the church. Mick's is a big family: there was Bernard, Patsy, Michael, Phyllis, John, Frankie, Raymond, Kathleen, Muriel, Mr and Mrs Clarke, Auntie Cissy, Uncle Bernie, Ninnie, and Mary and Hannah Sands. Oh my God, we had to do a relay! I got married in a tweedy blue costume with a pretty frilly blouse. My friend Maggie Gannon stood for me, and my brother Jackie gave me away. Bernie was best man. Michael and I didn't drink – we were too young; anyway; we didn't care too much for alcohol – but we spent the evening singing, and had a real knees-up. My family obviously caught the bug because our Jackie, Mickey and Nellie all married shortly afterwards, and there was more singing and dancing to be done.

Mick and I moved in with his parents. Their house was large, and we had a room upstairs. It wasn't all plain sailing. I wanted to make a nice little home for the two of us, so I bought an electric cooker. Every time Michael tried to connect it, he fused all the lights and his father would bang on: 'I knew you'd do this. Never mind that cooker, come down here and use ours.' Eventually I had to give in, but I had a terrible temper and caused all kinds of rows. I'm very stubborn, and their refusal to give in to me was a challenge; we had quite a few battles in the early months.

After I got married, I went to work for Vernons Pools, but I wasn't there very long. In April 1949 my son Michael was born. (I suppose everyone's totting up the dates now.) I was thrilled, but I was so ignorant about giving birth. The whole thing was bewildering, because nobody told you anything and I was only nineteen. I'd had labour pains all night, and I went into hospital at about five o'clock in the morning. He was only five pounds eight ounces when he was born, and he was put into the nursery straight away. I didn't see him until the following day. I was upset and crying. 'There's something wrong – why haven't they brought him to me?' The Sister had some compassion, and went to fetch him. It was devastating the way newborn babies were separated from their mothers in those days, and the way mothers were isolated – I was in hospital for a fortnight, and I was allowed only two visitors during the whole period.

It was hard going with a new baby and without the facilities people have now: we didn't have washing machines, and I seemed to be endlessly soaking terry towelling nappies. What's more, the nappies held water and babies got cold, lying in wet nappies in a wet cot. Grandma Clarke gave me a lot of help; she idolised Michael, her first grandchild. Michael was taken into hospital with acute bronchitis when he was four months old, and after that he didn't seem to develop as fast as I wanted him to. He had a tendency to be pernickety with his food, and I had a terrible time trying to feed him. He didn't improve until he had his tonsils out some years later, and his health really used to worry me.

When Michael was less than a year old, my sister Mary died. That was Mary, Lizzie and Dad, with only three years in between them. It was terribly sad watching Mary. She'd seen Lizzie suffer with TB and battle against the disease, prepared to try anything at all – but Lizzie lost the battle, so when her own illness was diagnosed as TB, Mary just gave up and didn't fight it. We were all with her when she died, so that was some consolation, though not much. She was only twenty-seven. It broke Mam's heart.

Despite my sadness, I had to think about the future. I was now pregnant with Kathleen, who was born in August 1950. She had a lovely chubby little face, and was very good; she didn't keep us awake very much, which was a real blessing.

When Kathleen was six months old I had to go back to work at Littlewoods because we needed the money. Grandma Clarke said that she would look after Michael, and Kathleen went into a nursery. Sometimes Mick would meet me from work and say, 'Don't let's go straight back, we'll go down to town. We'll be back in time to collect Kathleen.' He'd take me to Samson & Barlow's, a restaurant, and then we'd go to the pictures. We'd have to hightail it up to the nursery to pick Kathleen up, but it was wonderful to have those few snatched hours without responsibility.

By this time our room was feeling rather cramped; we wanted a place of our own, and some independence. I'd been trying to organise our accommodation since we were first married. The council had offered us an odd assortment of flats, none of which was suitable for a young family: there was a tenement, the first built in the whole of the country, and a very old and tiny flat, with landings running along outside. I went to see the priest and he said, 'Don't take anything unless it's got a bath in it.'

We refused four or five places before we were offered one in the tenements on Melrose Road, just behind the street where Mick's mother lived – on the top landing, which meant that I used to have to climb seventy-two stairs to reach our door, but I was absolutely delighted with it. It was a nice flat, with two bedrooms, a little kitchen and a small back room and hall: very basic, but there was hot water, a sink, and a draining board. We moved there in February 1952, and were very excited at the prospect of having our own place.

That year I got pregnant with Marion. I worked until five weeks before she was born, and my friends at Littlewoods helped me to keep going so long by doing my share of the heavy work: the stencil trays and metal plates we had to lift took some manoeuvring. When I think of it now, I was a bit stupid on the day I went into labour. I was going to have the baby at home, so everything had to be just so, and ready for the nurse. I went down to the communal wash-house. It was more than just a wash-house, it was like a meeting-place as well. I had slight labour pains, but I knew I had to get the washing done and I did so. Somebody else carried it back upstairs for me, otherwise I don't know how I would have managed. That May night the midwife brought Marion into the world.

Then I found out I was pregnant again. I thought: If I've got three, another one's not going to make that much difference, but I didn't tell Mam. On 25 May

1954, a year after Marion was born, I had Margi. That morning I was down at the wash-house again, then I came home and scrubbed the floors. I was on my knees when the nurse arrived. I'd had pains earlier that day, and sent Marion round to Mam. When I went into labour, Marion was still there, and no one had gone to fetch her. Mick couldn't go down there; he was on night work at the docks and couldn't afford to miss his shift; we needed the money badly. At about ten o'clock there was a knock at the door, and Mam was standing there with Marion. 'What's our Frances thinking about? Look at this poor little child out at this hour. I thought she'd come round for her. Where is she, Michael?'

He pointed at the bedroom. 'Oh my God!' she said. 'God bless you, is everything all right?'

Mick had to go to work and so Mam busied round. She couldn't do enough for us, but no sooner had she got Marion tucked into her cot than the lights went out. Panic stations! I gave Mam a shilling for the meter, but out in the dark hallway she started shouting, 'I can't get the shilling in. God bless us! What am I going to do?' I was stuck in bed and couldn't move, so she opened the door and collared a girl who was walking along the landing. 'Come in here. My poor lass has just had a baby and I can't get the shilling in the light.'

Margi was christened Margaret Mary. She says now that she thought we gave her those names because I thought she was going to be a nun! She was a very lively child, always wanting to be on the go, whereas Marion was placid and contented. That was just as well, because with four tiny children I had my hands full, even though Michael spent a lot of time at his grandma's. I'd go downstairs with two of them in the pram and Kathleen walking beside me. She was like a little mother – she liked to be in charge, and knowing that she was the eldest daughter, she took authority, even at an early age. She was very quick to pick things up, our Kathleen.

I'd take them along to Stanley Road to do the shopping. In the early 1950s, one of the first people to find out that you were pregnant was the butcher, because you were issued with a green ration book to prove your condition and get your extra rations. The family allowance was a boon too. We always maintained that our children were born on Tuesdays because that meant they were entitled to the allowance for that week. I don't think there were many kids in our area who were born on a different day. The family allowance didn't always stretch far enough. Sometimes I'd have vegetables from the local shop on trust until Fridays, when Mick got paid, but I never felt pressurised by that. It was a lovely area; everyone knew everyone else and they were really helpful, they'd assist in any way they could. But it was hard going at times. I'd drag the kids, the shopping bags and the pram back up the seventy-two stairs to the flat, then discover I'd run out of salt. I often wished I could abseil.

It wasn't always easy to get out and about, and the wash-house was one of the most popular meeting-places in the area, where I'd see friends of my own age, all with babies in tow, and we'd have a chat and a laugh as well as getting the washing done. It was like a community centre. I always reckon that Liverpool was the first city to have wash-houses; they were started by Kitty Wilkinson in the 1800s and provided stalls for hand-washing. By my day, fortunately, machines had been installed.

You had to book a machine in advance, then take your turn in the queue. You had to get there early because the place would be packed out, and sometimes you'd be on pins in case you couldn't get in. For a shilling, or maybe one and six, you bought a ticket for two hours – that gave you the use of a stall containing a sink, a soaking-tub, a draining-board, a boiler and a machine. When you'd done your washing, you dried it by pushing great steel rods, called maidens, on to the clothing, then moved on to the ironing room. The wash-houses were a godsend because you needn't have dirty clothes piled up or clean, wet ones hanging around the flat – everything would be done and dusted within the day, and all for a few coppers.

Money was often tight, but it became nigh-on impossible to manage during a six-week dock strike in 1955, when there was no money coming in at all. I supported the strike. I would never have stopped Mick striking for the benefit of the workers, nor force him to walk across a picket line – which he wouldn't have done anyway. I wouldn't pressurise him into doing something that I thought abhorrent. After all was said and done, they were getting only a pittance of a wage on the docks. The Dock Board was making a considerable amount of money, and these men were working hard, five and a half days a week, till seven o'clock at night to make any sort of living wage. Even though it was going to be difficult with the kids, I told Mick we'd get by.

Mick had never been what they call 'stuck down' with his money; there was never an amount set aside for him and one for me: we shared a common purse. But the strike almost caused ructions. A man along the landing, also a docker, said to Mick, 'Go to the DHSS and tell them you've got young children and you'll get a few bob to last the week, so that you can get a few things in.'

He came back and told me, 'They've only given me two quid.'

'We'll manage, we'll be all right,' I said. He gave me the two pounds, and I went to the shops.

I always stopped off at Grandma's (Mick's mother's) on the way back, and she'd have a cup of tea and an egg on toast, or something for me. On this occasion, Margi, who was only a toddler, ran along Grandma's lobby and her shoes came off. I went along after her and sat her on the stairs to put them back on. My hearing has always been perfect – I can hear a pin drop at a hundred yards – and from the edge of the lobby I heard Mick's brother John saying, 'Is that all they give you, our kid, three pounds?' I said to myself: Three pounds? He said only two.

I ran straight in and demanded, 'How much did you get?' When he said 'Three,' I caused absolute murder! Grandma took my part, but Mick hadn't done it because he was trying to get one over on me, he said. 'I was keeping this pound in case you ran short.'

I believed him, because he was always a provider, whatever he had. All money went into the house, for me and the kids. Even so, I wanted to let him know I'd heard that he'd kept some money back. When you think of it now, it's extraordinary. You can't even give a child a pound – they'd say 'What can you get with that?' But it was a considerable amount then.

We kept going somehow through the strike. We may have missed paying the rent for a few weeks, and times were hard in some respects, but when I look back, those trials were part and parcel of life.

In September of the same year Frank, our second son, was born. There were several of us on the landing who were pregnant at the same time, and we all used to joke that the same feller was responsible. One of the women, Nellie, always took to her bed when she was pregnant, and the rest of us waited on her. This time, pregnant myself, I ran down the stairs to fetch the nurse for Nellie, and the next day it was my turn. I'd called in to see how Nellie was doing, and fortunately the nurse had done the same. She told me to get straight back home, and just over an hour later Frank arrived.

We had a few crises with the kids. One winter four of them caught whooping cough. I slept with two of the children, and Mick had to sleep with the other two to make sure they were all right during the night. They hadn't been up and about very long when Margi and Marion caught pneumonia – just before Christmas. That winter was a real hurdle, but it couldn't prepare me for the following year.

In July 1957 I gave birth to Joan; she was beautiful, with deep-set blue eyes and auburn hair, but at the age of four and a half months she died of pneumonia. Her death practically destroyed me. I'll never forget it, or her; it was an experience that was so devastating I didn't know how I was going to survive. The other children all knew, and felt my grief, even though they were only small themselves. Joan was the first of my children to die; I still feel sad when I think of her.

· 5 ·

Born Aged Twenty-nine:
The Move to Kirkby

I've always said that I was born aged twenty-nine – that's the age I was when we moved to Kirkby, where we've lived ever since. The tenement flat had become a bit of a squeeze, and I'd put my name down on the housing list for something larger. Everyone in the tenements wanted to move to an area called Fazakerley, and at the time, very few people wanted to go to the new town of Kirkby, which was eight miles outside Liverpool. But it was Kirkby that we were offered.

Two months earlier, in September 1958, I'd given birth to Eileen. She was a demanding baby, with a real will of her own – she still has that – and with a growing family, I could see that it was time to move for the sake of the children. Mick didn't really like the idea because it would be a bit of a hardship for us. In the tenements the rent was 8s. 2d. a week; in Kirkby it would be 29s. 9d., which made it over three times as expensive. Additionally, it would cost him an extra half a crown a day to get down to the docks. But I couldn't see any future for the children, living on the top landing of a tenement block. I thought: We'll go. We've managed before, we'll manage again. That Rodgers and Hammerstein song, 'A Cockeyed Optimist', could have been written about me.

My brother's mates worked for a produce firm, and offered to lend us the wagon. 'We'll move you, love,' they said, and sure enough they arrived at the door with a van that usually stored potatoes and cabbages. We were like the Clampetts of the 'Beverly Hillbillies', the only thing missing was a rocking chair – we couldn't afford one. All the furniture was piled up, and we set off for Kirkby. I knew right away that it was going to be the place for me.

We moved into a three-bedroomed house on Didsbury Close, by the main road. With an extra bedroom and a small morning-room, I was excited by our new home. If you looked at it now, you'd ask why architects built houses like that. They had *carte blanche* to build homes suitable for families, and especially large families like mine, but it wasn't three-bedroomed as they'd claimed; you could only just get a small single bed in one of the rooms. To try to counteract the problem, I bought bunk beds. But a bigger problem was the bare walls. The houses had only just been built and hadn't had time to dry out, so the plaster was cold and damp. No one could do any decorating, and it was difficult to keep warm when the rooms and water were heated by a coal fire downstairs. It was a terrible winter, and within a couple of months Eileen was taken ill and had to be hospitalised for six weeks.

Because we'd been offered a house, it was like manna from heaven to have one, but they'd been built on the cheap, simply thrown together, and outside there were no pavements; workmen were still building walls and hanging doors. There were no facilities either. The nearest shops to the housing estate were at Quarry Green, half a mile away. There was a chip shop, a bakery, a newsagent's, a hairdresser's, a greengrocer's and a chemist's, and that was our lot. Along with the mobile vans – which we relied on – they had to serve something like a thousand people. Kirkby town centre wasn't built until the 1960s, by which time Kirkby had the highest population under the age of twenty-one in the whole of Western Europe. We were so thrilled to have a house that we put up with the terrible inconveniences, but I don't think we should have done. We'd been moved into an area that wasn't yet fit for people to live in, let alone people with young families, like most of us. It seemed that because we were the working classes, anything was good enough for us.

From the very beginning, money was pretty desperate. We were fortunate in many respects, because my mam had the handcart and could supply us with fruit and vegetables. Whenever I went to see her she'd say, 'Go and sort out what's in the yard and take it home,' and Mick's mother would bring all sorts of things for us. The whole family jogged in, and though we had to skip paying the Provident once in a while and run up an amount on the slate, we managed to get by. We were always trying to find ways and means of surviving, but at least everyone else was in the same position.

My friend Mary used to tell of a woman whose husband would dig the garden to plant seed potatoes. After he'd gone to work, his wife would dig them up again to cook for tea. Her husband didn't realise that their money was so scarce that this was the only way she was able to feed the kids. He could never understand why everyone else's garden had loads of potatoes, and although he'd bought the best variety, he never had a crop!

There were days when we'd say, 'Oh God, what can I do to get a decent meal?' And we'd rack our brains to think of something that was nourishing. A butcher used to come round, but he didn't last long because no one could pay him, and at times the coalman's visits were infrequent because not enough people were settling their bills. It wasn't because they didn't want to pay, they simply didn't have the money.

The kids loved Kirkby because there were plenty of open spaces for them to play in, but Mick missed being near his family, and wasn't happy until they moved there as well. It took us a while to settle in, and it was hard going at first because we didn't know anyone. The children made friends at school, and through them we got to know their mothers. In a group of people you soon find the ones who are sympathetic to your ideology and your sense of humour, and four of us – Mary, Rene, Teresa and I – became close friends. All I've ever had to do is pick up the phone and they've been there on the double, and the same with me, if they need me.

There was nowhere for us to go because we never had any money, so we'd go to each other's houses and have a giggle over different things. Rene was a great

Frances, aged 12, with her mother and brother Teddy, taken in Cardigan during one of Frances' mother's visits to her reluctant evacuees.

The corner of Great Homer Street and Roscommon Street (on the right), Frances' childhood home; this photograph was taken in 1964 when cars, rather than shire horses, had begun to make their mark.

Everton Brow, 1927. Frances used to play here on the way to visit her married sister Lizzie.

A row of handcarts, outside Wheelrights of Skirving Street, similar to those which Frances' mother pushed to Bootle's Strand Road and back, for over 60 years.

Liverpool women on the way to the wash house, 1952, carrying their laundry on their heads, as Frances' mother did for many years.

Frances and her brother, Teddy, in the backyard of their mother's Sackville Street house, early 1950s.

Above: Three of Frances' children (left to right): Jane, Muriel and Eileen, posing at home in the early 1960s.

Left: Frances with Michael, aged 2½, and Kathleen, aged 9 months, at the back of Roscommon Street, 1951.

The Clarke family, en route to a wedding in 1964. Back row: Nellie (Frances' sister), Marion, Mick, Kathleen, Frances, holding Muriel, Michael. Front row: Eileen, Frank, Margi, Ann (cousin, in front), Jane.

Marion holding Angela, with Frank peeping over the hedge and Muriel in the doorway of Didsbury Close, Kirkby, 1968.

Frances' political debut – the photograph that launched the Dissatisfied Residents Action Group (DRAG), early 1970s.

Frank, Margi and Alexandra Pigg: photo call during the making of Letter to Brezhnev, *1985.*

The Mayor of Knowsley swings into action: Frances takes the controls to launch the demolition of a block of maisonettes in Whitefield Ward.

Above: Frances as newly appointed Mayor of Knowsley, 1991.

Right: Frances.

Cardigan revisited: Frances and her friend, Nancy Newcombe, 1992, leaning against the cannon that was a meeting point for the evacuees.

organiser. She'd say, 'In four weeks' time, we'll all have a day out,' and in the meantime, instead of paying what we owed to Annie the moneylender, we'd put a few coppers aside towards the double-decker bus that Rene would hire from the Corporation. I remember one embarrassing occasion when we were sitting on West Kirkby beach and who should we see but Annie, who we'd been dodging for weeks. We had to move sharpish.

A whole gang of us would get together, and Rene would work out how many people were going on the trip. A mother, father or another adult had to be in charge of their children, because it was a family occasion. Rene would put three children on a seat, and calculate how much the seat was for two, and divide that so that the children paid less. Anyone with four children travelled as cheaply as someone with two; those with big families were subsidised. It always worked out, and we were all delighted. No one could afford to go on holiday, so we relied on Rene's days out.

I remember one visit to the open-air swimming baths at West Kirkby beach. I was a bit of a joker, and after my swim I jumped out of the water and put on a dressing-gown. It was ripped from under the arm to the floor, and everyone was laughing at me, but my face was deadpan. I gave them a look of disdain and walked towards the café.

When Mary saw me, she fell about. 'Excuse me, dear, are you laughing at me?' I said, in my coolest voice.

She couldn't answer, and the café went quiet.

'If you think you're going to stand there and laugh at me, you've got another think coming.'

Mary played along with me – she knew I was only acting the goat, although the others in the café didn't know we were friends.

'What are you going to do about it?' she said.

'You come downstairs and I'll show you.' The tension in the café was high – even the waitresses were listening, expecting an explosion. Outside, just around the corner, we doubled up with laughter.

Along the promenade was a row of alcoves with covered seats, where people would sit and watch the ships coming up the Mersey. The day was turning overcast, and now that the kids had had a swim they were beginning to get bored. 'Tell you what, we'll have a concert,' I said. There were half a dozen elderly people sitting on the prom, and we asked them to be our audience. They were hesitant at first, because we were a bit brash, but in the end we persuaded them. 'Come on, we'll sing the old songs and you can reminisce about when you were courting.' We sat them down in the alcove and shared out our sandwiches, saying, 'Eat up. You're our ninnies.' (Ninny is a Liverpool word for grandma.) Then the concert began. All the music-hall songs were rolled out, and they joined in with the singsong. Unless they got some extraordinary nourishment from the sandwiches we gave them, they'll all have been long since dead, but they had a good laugh that afternoon.

They were lovely days out, and they didn't cost the earth. We all mucked in together and made our own entertainment. We'd arrive home exhausted, and then begin the business of cleaning out the bus. Rene was in charge, and she insisted that we make a good impression on the youngsters – woe betide anyone who left litter beneath their seat.

When we'd all settled in, and Eileen was a toddler, I looked for some work that I could fit in around the kids, and found myself a couple of jobs. I'd go into Liverpool at 6.30 in the morning and clean two offices before catching the bus back for 8.15 to take the children to school. Then I'd hightail it down to the chemist's, where I was also a cleaner. The chemist's shop was a new building, and had to be spick and span – it was a down-on-your-knees job, not a mop-and-bucket one. For two hours every morning I scrubbed that shop from top to toe. It was hard work, but Mrs Kay was a good employer and very generous, as was Mrs Morrison, who also worked there, and really helped me. It was the tradition at Christmas for the kids to have new clothes, and I was always trying to figure out how to manage that. Mrs Morrison, who was an avid knitter, asked if she could make anything for me. At Christmas she presented me with pullovers for Michael and Frank and a cardigan for each of the four girls, and refused to take any money.

In July 1961 Jane was born, my first true Kirkbyite. She was born with a caul – a kind of veil – over her face, which people always said was a lucky omen: an angel mask, which meant that the child would never want. (I don't know whether our Jane would agree with that now!) But she was lucky in many respects, and has a lovely personality. She was no trouble – I always say that I had Jane to keep me from going insane with the rest of them! Of course I couldn't go back to work, but Mick used to help me around the house, which eased things. Sometimes, if I couldn't get out to the wash-house, we'd do the washing at the sink and Mick would wring out the clothes for me, while we sang all the Jimmy Rogers songs. I'd be singing seconds, and he'd be yodelling. When we think back now, we say times were hard, but we really did have a lovely life.

A year later, in December, Muriel was born. I went into hospital at half-past ten at night and she was born at ten to twelve; the nurse couldn't get over it. The winter that followed was the worst on record. When I brought Muriel home, I had to stay on the settee in the living-room. We couldn't take her upstairs because the rooms were so cold. Mick brought one of the bunk beds downstairs and I used to sleep in the little parlour with her; we had to have the fire lit all night because the weather was so terrible. Muriel was only just over six pounds when she was born, so of course she was fussed over. She and Jane were always very close, because they grew up together as babies, although all the children were good friends. But it was Kathleen who was the enormous help. When a woman like me has daughters, the eldest is like a confidante, and although Kathleen was only twelve when Muriel was born, she took over the house and tried to do what she could. She was very domineering, and used to shout at us and keep us all in check; we used to call her bossy-boots. But she was a really sensible girl, and a second mother to the others.

On Saturday nights, Mick's brothers used to take him out, but it was rare for me to join them – there was always too much to do. All the children had to be bathed, and the girls had to have their hair put in ringlets for Mass the next day. I wouldn't allow any of them to stay in bed, although on the day Margi made her First Communion, Frank was left behind, in disgrace.

I was getting myself and everyone else ready, and Frank kept getting in the way. I was saying, 'You get those shoes on, find some socks, you put those shoes on.'

In the midst of all this turmoil, I saw Frank – who was only a little boy – tiptoeing back upstairs. 'Clock's broke,' he said, 'but I haven't broke it.'

Sure enough, the glass was broken. 'You little so and so,' I shouted. 'Get back up to bed.'

I told Mick, 'Keep him upstairs, he's not coming with us.'

When we came back from the Holy Communion breakfast, we discovered that Frank had come back downstairs and broken the fingers on the clock as well. It was ages before we got a new one, and Mick and I were the only ones who were tall enough to tell the time by walking right up to the face and peering at its little stumpy fingers.

·6·

Tragedy

In 1963 the Beatles hit Liverpool, and the city buzzed with the sound. The atmosphere in the city centre was phenomenal, and the excitement was contagious. It was *the* city to be in, and all the clubs were packed. Occasionally Mick and I went to the Cabaret Club with his brothers. My friend Chrissie would do my hair in a beehive and put all my make-up on. I remember some feller saying to Mick, 'Who's the dolly bird?' On the bus into town, people would sing at the top of their voices; we'd run through the Stones, the Beatles, Billy J. Kramer, the Searchers, the Merseybeats and Gerry and the Pacemakers – and this was just at the start of the evening. You should have heard the singing on the way back!

Kathleen and her friends were in seventh heaven. I remember her writing out a song and reciting, 'C'mon, c'mon, c'mon, c'mon . . .' to herself. 'What kind of lyrics are they?' I asked. It wasn't until I heard them sung to music that I realised how good they were.

We had a radio and had just got a television, but we didn't have a record-player. My brother Teddy, who was working in London, had left one at Mam's, so Kathleen wrote to ask if she could borrow it. 'Certainly,' came the reply, 'as long as you don't play anything by Arthur Askey, Alan Breeze or Billy Cotton.' She was always singing – although she had a shocking voice – and strains of 'You don't have to say you love me . . .' wafted through the house. Her uncle used to call her 'Dusty'.

Kathleen had always been mature for her age, and now she was thirteen she took a Saturday job on the market, for which she was paid ten bob. When she got home she'd say, 'Here y'are, Mother.'

'No, girl,' I'd say, 'you keep it and save up for some clothes.' But she'd insist that I had some of it, and was really pleased to be helping me.

Kathleen had a lovely manner, and the kids would fuss round her. 'Who'll go to the van' she'd ask, and they'd all say, 'Me'. She'd tell them what she could afford to buy and add, 'Get five Woodies for my dad.'

Kathleen was a keen netball player – she was captain of the school team, and she was always training and going to matches. She started to complain of a pain in her leg, which was swollen. 'You've probably strained it,' I said. 'Go over to the doctor's and get him to have a look.'

When she came back, Kathleen said, 'I've got to go to the hospital. The doctor thinks it's fluid.'

At the hospital the doctor told Mick and me that he wanted to keep her in. 'In ninety per cent of cases like this it's just fluid on the bone. But in the other ten per cent it's a tumour.' Our hearts stopped for some moments.

She had an operation, and was in hospital for a fort-night. Everyone went to visit her. Then, on a Saturday night when Mick was working (he was on the buses by this time), I went in to see Kathleen by myself. Before I saw her, the Sister called me into the office and said, 'I'm sorry to tell you, but your daughter has a tumour on the bone. They might have to take her leg off.' I was stunned, but I had to keep calm, although I felt hysterical.

I went into Kathleen, and when she asked, 'What did they say?' I said, 'It's only fluid, and they've got to wait for it to come to a head before they can drain it off.'

I came out of the hospital in a daze and went to the first church I came to, and into confession. The priest was really compassionate and tried to console me, but I couldn't be consoled. We were devastated; we didn't know what had hit us.

Mick and I were sent to the Royal Infirmary and saw the professor, Mr Malone. I can see him now, sitting on the edge of the examination table, looking down at us.

'I'm sorry,' he said, 'there's nothing we can do for your daughter. We can only take her leg off to relieve her pain.'

We just sat there; we didn't know what to say.

'I don't believe you,' I said.

'I'm sorry, I'm telling you the truth. Your daughter will be dead in a fortnight.'

'Do you mean to tell me that nothing can be done for a young, healthy girl, who's never been sick for a day in her life? There must be something you can do.'

'No, there isn't. I'm sorry.'

I just kept saying, 'I don't believe you.'

It was the 13th of April 1965. Michael's brother Patsy and my sister Nellie were waiting for us when we came out, and I told them, 'There's nothing they can do. We'll bring her home. There we can at least give her all our love and whatever she wants.'

We brought Kathleen home. 'How long do you think it will be before this thing comes to a head?' she asked.

'It shouldn't be long, girl.'

There was no way that we could tell her the truth – she was concerned about her health anyway, and wouldn't have been able to cope with such terrible news. She was only fifteen. As there was nothing the medical profession could do, we had to make our own decisions, and we won't ever know whether we made the right ones or not. But we did what we thought was right at the time.

We decided that Kathleen should go to Lourdes, and Patsy paid the bulk of the money for her and me to travel there. We flew to Bordeaux, with Kathleen dressed in lovely new clothes, then caught a train on to Lourdes. When we arrived, it was as if we were coming home. It's a feeling that's hard to describe. Kathleen couldn't carry any luggage because of her illness, but a helpful taxi driver found us a small hotel. All pilgrimages to the Lourdes bath were prearranged – you couldn't simply walk in, but had to be part of a group. And of course, we weren't.

I was getting desperate, but then I took a priest to one side and told him Kathleen's story. He took hold of both of us and led us in. As you enter, everyone says the rosary. You then remove your garments and go into the women's bath, continuing to recite. Two nuns drape you in a wet sheet that's so bitterly cold it takes your breath away, and moving down the bath, you make your way to the statue of Our Lady, kneel down and kiss Our Lady's feet. As you kneel, you're completely submerged. Then you leave the bath right away and get dressed without drying yourself. What a wonderful experience that was. We were both moved by Lourdes. We then went to Gavarnie for a few days' holiday – both terrified by the hairpin bends *en route* to Pont Espanã, the highest peak in the Pyrenees, which Kathleen insisted we visit.

We returned to London on 5 May, the day Liverpool Football Club had battled their way through to the cup final at Wembley. It was a match that everyone wanted to be at, and our Teddy had bought tickets for us. But Kathleen was tired and in pain, and wanted to go home. Liverpool won the cup, and the next day we took Kathleen to see their triumphant homecoming. She was in high spirits, because we'd assured her that she wouldn't have to go back into hospital.

One of Mick's brothers, Frankie, was living in New York, and he sent tickets to Kathleen and his sister Muriel so that they could visit him. They had a marvellous time and were taken to theatres and dances all over town. At Arthur's Restaurant Kathleen collected film stars' autographs and generally lapped up the glitzy atmosphere. Everyone made a fuss of her and treated her as if she was the only girl in town, because they knew she was dying.

There was no end to the kindness people showed on Kathleen's behalf: all our friends and family thought about ways to make her happy. Kathleen's big love was, of course, music. A friend of mine knew someone who was married to one of the Pacemakers, and arranged for Kathleen and a friend to spend a day at Blackpool with Gerry Marsden and the band. He was very considerate; he took her all round the theatre and introduced her to Gene Vincent, who was appearing on the same show. It was an important day for Kathleen. We never had the opportunity to thank Gerry Marsden, but Mick and I are really grateful to him.

In the September a notice appeared in the paper advertising the Rolling Stones at the Liverpool Empire. Kathleen, her four friends and her cousin were all crackers about the Rolling Stones. She said, 'Oh Mother, you must get me tickets to go.' I didn't know how I was going to manage it, but by hook or by crook I was determined to get those tickets.

I sent a letter to the manager of the Empire, writing about Kathleen in such a way as to arouse his curiosity without telling him the full story. His reply asked me to go down and see him. When I explained about her disability and how she couldn't sit in an ordinary seat in case someone knocked her leg, he said, 'You can have the royal box.' That man was lovely. I paid for it, of course, but only the standard seat price. The royal box held only four, so I also bought two seats in the stalls.

When I told Kathleen, she was over the moon. Grandma Clarke bought her a blue suede coat for the occasion, and one of Teddy's mates drove the girls to the Empire in a huge limousine – they travelled in style. They'd left the house looking like models, but when Mick went to collect them, all their mascara had run down their faces, which were streaked with tears of excitement. He walked up to the box and said, 'Come on, girl.'

'Where are we going, Dad?' she said. And he carried her down the stairs, across the stage and to the dressing-room.

Kathleen was just overcome. When she got there, she said, 'Dad, put me down, put me down. I'm walking in.'

'There was Mick Jagger, Brian Jones, Bill Wyman and Keith Richards.

'Go and get Charlie,' said Mick Jagger. 'Kathleen wants to see Charlie.' He then turned to her and said, 'Do you smoke, Kathy?' She said no. 'Do you want a Coke?' She took the Coke, and got their autographs. I'll always remember her dad telling me that when they came out of the stage door and walked into a mass of screaming girls, someone said, '*She*'s been to see the Rolling Stones. Oh, I wish I was her.'

That evening gave my lovely daughter an immense pleasure that lived with her through the next difficult months. She got steadily worse – it's almost too painful, too sad, to remember. When Christmas came, she was in bed. The bone specialist came to the house two or three times, and a nurse called regularly, as did the nuns from the nearby convent. Our Teddy would walk into the room and say, 'Sister, didn't I see you in *The Sound of Music*?' They used to laugh.

Sister Kenneth, the cook, was a frequent visitor. As I opened the front door to her she'd hold out two carrier bags. 'This is for you, Mrs Clarke. I know you've got a lot of mouths to feed, and visitors. Don't say nothing.' She'd bring all sorts: butter, tea, sugar, cakes, soda bread. We always had a bit of a joke about the soda bread, because nobody really liked it and it used to go as hard as rock.

The house was always full, but I had to ask people not to stay long because it tired Kathleen, and the vibration of anyone entering her room caused her terrible pain. When she had to be moved, it was agony for her. Once, our Michael ran out of the house; I left too, because I couldn't stand listening to her. The first person I met on the street was my friend Mary. I was crying, and she started crying too because a few years before she'd lost her own son from a brain tumour, so she knew what we were going through.

In April 1966 Kathleen died. It was a traumatic period. We'd seen her go through some great suffering, and it's hard to explain the loss we felt. I had my faith, but Mick's was less strong. 'She's in the arms of Our Lord now,' I said. 'He's loving and comforting her.' That gave me some sustenance, which I passed on to Mick, but the year disappeared in a blur of anguish.

· 7 ·

Adventure

Kathleen and Michael had always been very close; as the eldest children they had a particular rapport, and her death was a terrific blow to him. Michael was one of those young lads who was always on the go – he was an impulsive person who had to do everything immediately. When he was only fourteen he started bunking off school, and a month before he was due to leave, he was expelled. I was extremely worried by the effect this would have on Michael's ability to get a job, and went to see his headmaster. Fortunately – although Michael didn't thank me – he was reinstated.

He was swept along with the tide of the 1960s, the sense that you could do whatever you wanted without restriction. Michael took that literally. He caused us a great deal of heartache because he'd go missing and we'd be searching everywhere for him, wondering what danger he was in. And he did get into all sorts.

I remember a policeman calling at our house and saying, 'Your son Michael is in London's Cannon Row police station.' My brother Teddy was working as a stage hand at the Lyric Theatre, so I asked him to collect Michael and give him a good talking-to. Teddy threatened him with dire consequences if he didn't go straight back to Liverpool, and put Michael on the train. But Michael got off at the next station. That's the kind of harum-scarum lad he was.

In the year after Kathleen's death he became even more restless: he was in and out of mischief, and we knew that unless he was presented with some kind of opportunity, he'd end up doing some porridge. A job came up on a Cunard ship, sailing to America. Michael was fascinated by the States – he'd always wanted to go. He had no experience of sailing, but he was desperate to get the job. Our friend Joe Concannon wrote him a reference and, armed with this, Michael was taken on. Mick, Joe Concannon and his uncle Frankie went down to see him off.

The crossing from Liverpool to New York took seven days, and it was really rough. Michael was seasick all the way, but when the ship docked in New York, he was in high spirits. He was only seventeen, so the ship's company was responsible for him. He went to the captain and coaxed a sub from him. Michael was always a charmer – like the character Nigel Havers played on the television – and he had a very winning personality. He obviously charmed the captain. With some money in his pocket, Michael left the ship. He stayed in New York for two days, then hitchhiked to Azle in Texas. That's some feat. Meanwhile, Cunard was being fined because the ship couldn't leave without him . . .

Some years earlier, on one of his jaunts to London, Michael had befriended a Texan family, the Whites, and now he tracked them down. He stayed with the Whites, and they were delighted with him. In fact the whole of Azle seemed to be. A Mrs Crabtree wrote to ask if I would agree to Michael being legally adopted by her! Of course I wouldn't have allowed that, but it shows the esteem in which he was held by the community. It was a Baptist town in the Bible belt, and they were all dedicated people.

Then Michael was up and off. I said to Mick, 'I know where he's gone – he's gone to San Francisco for the flower power.' And sure enough, he hitchhiked to San Francisco, where he was in his element. It was just a dream come true for him. He wanted to stay in the States, but he made the mistake of returning to Azle, where he was arrested as an illegal immigrant. He was put in San Antonio jail, then deported. Our Michael was only five foot eight, and two burly, six-foot-four FBI men put him on the plane. Understandably, the stewardesses were wary of him until they found out that he was only an illegal immigrant, not a dangerous criminal. Then they fussed over him.

The plane touched down in New Orleans, and Michael even made an effort to get off again. Of course the stewardess said, 'If it was in my power I'd let you go, but it's more than my job's worth.' He came back from New York by ship. When it docked at Liverpool I went down to meet him; I was determined to be there in case anything untoward happened, but everything was all right and the police brought him home. It was all just a big adventure to Michael, who thought that the only thing he'd done wrong was to return to Texas. He was really ahead of his time, too fast and too eager.

When he returned, Michael fell back into his old ways, got himself into trouble, and was arrested. Mick hitchhiked from Liverpool to London to be with his son when he went before the magistrates. They knew all the background circumstances, and were really very good. They said to Mick, 'How did you get down?' and when he said, 'I hitched,' they told him, 'You won't hitchhike back.' They gave him train vouchers, and said to Michael, 'Now go home.' People didn't realise how difficult it was for Michael, because he'd idolised Kathleen, his younger sister. The two of them were always together, and as I've said, her illness and death had a devastating effect on him.

At the end of 1967 I found out that I was pregnant. We were thrilled, because although we already had a big family, we felt that this would be some recompense for the loss of Kathleen. But I was thirty-eight, and this would be my tenth child. I suffered from toxaemia, and wasn't well; I was in and out of hospital throughout. I used to have all the other expectant mothers laughing. The nurse would say, 'You're better than all the needles, to bring on a labour. We had six of them down last week, sent into labour because you made them laugh so much.'

While I was in hospital, Marion was put in charge of the house. She was fifteen and she did a marvellous job, but it was less easy for her to take charge of the other kids. Margi was always a live wire, and she'd be bunking off school, with four or five other girls, and taking them home. On one occasion Catherine, my eldest sister, went to see if Marion was getting on all right and, despite her protestations, went upstairs to open the windows to air the house. There she discovered a foot sticking out from under a bed, from which several guilty schoolgirls emerged.

My tenth baby was born in March 1968. She had rosy cheeks and a good pair of lungs; she screamed. I couldn't, because my throat had seized up, and I was choking, but nobody realised. As soon as that drama was over, I looked at my beautiful baby. Her brother Michael asked me to call her Angela because she was brought by the angels, so I did. With Angela we settled into a thanksgiving. She wasn't a replacement for Kathleen, of course, she was a personality in her own right, but her birth did much to reduce our mourning.

Almost as soon as I was discharged from hospital, Mick announced that the buses were going on strike. Oh Lord! They were out for something like eleven weeks, but they say it's an ill wind that blows nobody any good. For all that time, Angela stayed downstairs in her cot and I slept undisturbed; Mick looked after her during the night.

Mick has always been good with his children – he adores them. He's very sympathetic and really soft-hearted. His children are THE children, and he'd stand by them, no matter what. In fact I sometimes say, 'I wish I was your daughter. I'd get more done for me then!'

· 8 ·

The Fun and Games Begin: Early Politics

In 1969 the fun and games began. One evening I went round to Rene's house with Mary and Teresa. We were all Labour supporters, and always have been. The three of us were reared on politics. My brothers and sisters were always talking politics and even when I was young, and thinking about the next dance, I was conscious that Labour was the Party for me. In the area of Liverpool where I grew up, where you'd see people who were destitute or living from hand to mouth, you couldn't but be aware that there was a lot of inequality. I remember the excitement of the Labour victory after the war and the promise that the Beveridge plan held. Thank God, we thought, now there'll be a decent life for everyone.

Much of our politics were humanitarian, I suppose. We'd been brought up in a community in which neighbours helped one another, and that spirit has always been strong in us. This particular evening we all got up in arms about the swimming baths which were being built in Kirkby. Our children had to travel to Liverpool if they wanted to go to the swimming baths. It cost 9d. to get in, and the bus fare was also 9d. – a total of 1s.6d.

I could afford to send only two children at a time, but they could stay in the pool all day if they wanted to, so it was good value for money. But it was quite a journey for children to make, and we were all delighted that Kirkby was finally going to have its own pool.

We weren't so delighted about the cost. 'Have you read the *Kirkby Reporter*?' asked Mary. 'The baths are opening shortly, and they're charging 1s.6d.'

We didn't realise at the time that the council had to pay back the loans they'd incurred in building the baths – all we saw was the need for young children to have facilities at a reasonable price, and we were furious that they'd have to pay the same amount to swim locally as they did to go into the city. One and sixpence seems like a pittance now – it's only about twelve pence – but it wasn't to us.

'What's worse', said Mary, 'is that they can only swim for half an hour.'

'We've got to do something about this,' said Rene. She was the head, the one with the know-how who, given the germ of an idea, would act on it.

The next day, Rene's daughter came round to my house. 'Mrs Clarke, my mam wants you.' Rene's health was always fragile, although she battled against it all along the line, and so I ran round to see her, thinking she must be ill.

When I got there, Rene said, 'Here y'are, Fran, sign this form. We're going to oppose the council, and set our own rate. The elections are in four weeks' time, and if we can get our nomination in now, we'll be able to challenge the council and highlight the injustice of the cost of the baths.'

I signed the form, saying, 'Is this a sort of protest?'

'Oh no,' she replied, 'we're putting our own candidate up for the election.'

'Who's the candidate?'

'You are. You just signed.'

I was staggered, but Rene was always a determined woman, so I went along with it. She did all the spade work, like an agent, and put my papers into the council. We needed ten signatures from the ward we hoped to represent. Nine of these came from women, and one from Rene's husband. We then needed a name for our party. We spent an evening mulling this over, and someone suggested that we should call ourselves the Dissatisfied Residents' Action Group. It sounded important so we said yes, that's it. It wasn't until we got the registration forms back that we realised what the initials spelled.

Rene produced and printed a leaflet that highlighted what we felt was wrong in Kirkby, and our Michael took me to get my photograph taken for the front. He was a little bit proud of me – I don't know if he realised that this was the start of something big! The other men didn't really want to know – this was simply something that the women were getting up to. Two to three thousand leaflets were delivered to Rene's, and all the women who'd signed the nomination turned up every night to distribute them. One woman kept coming back with more leaflets than she'd left with. 'Oh,' she said, 'each time I tried to put leaflets through the letterbox, there'd be another jammed in it.' She was taking out the opposition leaflets and putting ours in.

We had such a laugh campaigning. One evening,

Mary had to go and buy some milk *en route*. She was a very convincing speaker and she was standing on one doorstep, vehemently explaining why we needed the couple's support, when we heard a smash: Mary had dropped the milk bottle. We ended up with a bucket of water and two sweeping brushes, cleaning this woman's step and picking up broken glass, but we got two votes at that house.

Rene and I decided that we should go into the centre of Kirkby to do our stuff. Just the two of us – what a political force to reckon with! We had the support of some of the dockers, and one of them had given us a loud-hailer, so we marched off to the market on a Saturday morning and Rene climbed up on top of a wall. She started blustering all over the place and I said, 'Oh Rene, give us that hailer.'

I started explaining what we wanted for Kirkby, how we needed someone to be the conscience of the people, and so on. We gathered quite a crowd. When we'd finished, a man came up and said, 'Here's a pound towards your campaign.' We thought that was brilliant. It was Tommy Staples, the Secretary of the Communist Party and a sincere campaigner for people in need. We were pleased to have his support – not that we were against the Labour Party, but we felt that our campaign was the only way to make a protest.

At this time, Angela was about eight months old and Rene's youngest, Gillian, was two. We'd go out in the evenings with Angela at the top of her pram, Gillian at the bottom, and the loud-hailer in between. What a way for a serious political party to go out canvassing: two women, with two babies in a pram that we called the Queen of the Road. We often look back and laugh at how naive we were.

On the evening of the vote, the Labour Party had its big guns out in Minstead Ward. As a vulnerable area, it had four or five cars patrolling to drum up support. We had just the one, driven by George, my niece's husband. He thought it was all a bit of a giggle, not something to be taken seriously. 'Yes, girls, OK, I'll drive the car.'

The whole thing did become a bit of a giggle. George had a two-door car, so we had to stick the loud-hailer out of the window and give our spiel from either the back seat or the one by the driver. We were shouting out our manifesto, but it seemed that wherever we went, we were followed – I don't know whether someone paid them or not – by an ice-cream van playing 'Popeye the Sailorman' and drowning out our message.

There were four candidates and, as we expected, John King, the Labour Party candidate, held his seat – but I was second. It was as much of a surprise to me as to anyone else! I think I got 300-odd votes, which wasn't bad for a four-week campaign. After the count we all had to thank the returning officer, and I said, 'Well, this is our first attempt, and there's no way we're going to be discouraged. We most certainly will be back next year and we'll have another go.'

We'd known all along that we weren't going to get in, but we'd taken control rather than sit back and let other people dictate to us and say, 'This is what you should have', whether Kirkby needed it or not. It was an exhilarating feeling. Having said that, I must admit that Kirkby Urban District Council did wonderful things for the area. They built those swimming baths, created a town centre and the market. Many other areas in the region had been well established long before Kirkby received the attention and facilities it warranted, so the UDC made real progress.

That was my introduction to positive campaigning, and it was a really exciting time. It gave us experience as well as a sense of achievement: it also got us noticed. We were invited to various functions – including the opening of the swimming baths – and when Harold Wilson (who was Prime Minister at the time) came to Kirkby, he told a local Labour member, 'You get those two women in the Party.'

Rene and I did join the Labour Party; she was the instigator really – I can't speak too highly of her talents. We began to attend ward meetings regularly, and that's how our next battle came about.

During the Heath administration many people opposed the iniquity of the Fair Rent Act, whereby council rent was assessed on the basis of a well-maintained house in a particular area, so that those with fewer amenities were penalised by having to pay a rent that didn't match the standard of their home. Additionally, the person earning the highest wage was deemed to be the council tenant, so the tenancy could pass to a son or daughter, even though their parents had been on the rent book for years. There was a concerted battle against this legislation throughout the country, and Rene, Mary, Teresa and myself were drawn into it. People turned out to public meetings in droves, to give vent to their feelings.

I was chosen to be one of the speakers for the ward of Northwood. Our platform was that we would pay our rent, but not the increase. Some wards decided not to pay any rent at all, but that wasn't our stance. My first big speech took me by surprise: once more I was thrown in at the deep end. The Northwood delegation attended a meeting at the Royal Liverpool Institute, and as we filed in, Tommy Staples was filling out a form.

'What's that for, Tommy?' I asked.

'This is to nominate anyone who wants to speak.'

'Are you going to speak, Tommy?'

'No, you are.'

'I can't,' I said. 'I've never spoken in a formal meeting. What am I going to say?'

'You'll think of something.'

The hall was packed with Merseyside people, all wanting to have their say, so the chairman said he'd have to take speakers at random. Danny Wallace from Bootle stood up and said, 'We've got everything organised here; no one in Bootle is going to pay any rent.' The whole audience rose and applauded him. The next speaker also supported non-payment, and then my name was called.

My knees turned to jelly, but I stood up and began: 'Thanks very much for calling my name out, Mr Chairman, but I'm not really a speaker, and haven't been involved in politics for as long as the other members here. I'm delighted that Danny Wallace has Bootle sewn up, and that Mickey Keating has the area over the bridge sorted out. Me and my mates have been walking round Kirkby since June [it was now

November] and if anyone doesn't believe me, have a look at my shoe.' I lifted up my foot for everyone to see that there was a hole in my shoe. The whole audience roared with laughter. I knew I was on safe ground, so I was able to go on and explain our policy.

That was the start of all kinds of speeches against the Fair Rent Act; there were meetings and marches all over Liverpool, and I was asked to speak at many of the rallies. Then, as now, I spoke off the cuff, letting my sense of humour come through whatever point I wanted to make. I think my 'ordinary' approach won people over to my point of view.

The rent strike came to an end because people gradually started paying off their arrears. If you wanted to move to a larger or smaller house, or transfer to a council property in a different street, you needed a clear rent book, so people had to consider their overall position.

The early 1970s provided plenty of opportunities for political activity. Some of the disputes began locally, such as the support of the Kirkby Manufacturing Enterprise, where the workers shut out the managers and took over the factory lock, stock and barrel, to establish one of the first manufacturing co-ops in England. Sadly, the odds were stacked against them, but they had support throughout Merseyside and elsewhere too. Likewise the Shrewsbury Pickets, the two from Merseyside who were arrested and imprisoned on a charge of conspiracy for secondary picketing. We all rallied to their cause, incensed at the injustice of their treatment. The Kirkby Labour Club organised a train so that we could go and demonstrate in London. What a journey that was – it felt like a real charabanc outing. We were all spurred on by a common cause, and when a group of Merseysiders get together, there's always a lot of laughter. I think Our Lord must have said, 'You're all going to have a tough time, it's going to be a struggle, but to counteract that, I'll give you a really good sense of humour.'

We marched from Euston to the House of Commons, where we joined a crowd of thousands. You were only allowed into the House with your constituent MP but, one way and another, several of us managed to get in. Though it wasn't the focus of the occasion, I remember my House of Commons cup of tea. Tate & Lyle were on strike at the time, and none of us had any sugar at home. When we left the canteen, Parliament was several cubes of sugar lighter!

The campaigns continued, and my involvement in local politics grew alongside. In 1976 I was selected as the candidate for the forthcoming election in the Whitefield Ward, Kirkby. I'd been selected a year earlier, but Walter Tomlinson, the Liberal councillor, retained his seat. This time I beat Wally by a tiny margin, and was elected councillor. I was delighted to win the seat. I've always been totally committed to socialism and the betterment of the class in society which has very little say, doesn't influence market forces, and whose people are used as cannon fodder, with industry as the cannon. Now I had the opportunity to fight for my beliefs and for Whitefield Ward. I think I did just that; I really put everything into it.

When you're a new councillor you're supposed to keep your mouth shut for twelve months, take in all the procedures and learn the ropes, but I opened my mouth at my first meeting. To give them their due, the officers of the council responded to me. They knew that I was an innocent abroad, and they listened to my comments. I'd started as I meant to go on, as an idealist. I'd been elected for four years, and there was a lot of council work to get on with. The problems of Whitefield were great. I don't think the rest of the country realise the difficulties the people of Kirkby face – not least the multitude of flats in a disgraceful state, and the high unemployment. People needed some support.

I enjoyed doing my surgery. I'd sit in Verley Road School every week, and people would come and ask my advice about housing, social services, the ombudsman, or whatever. There'd be about twenty or thirty people waiting to see me, and sometimes I'd be there from seven to until ten. I don't really think the person in the street realises how much time a local councillor gives to the community. It should be a full-time job for an elected representative, and I also think there should be some remuneration. If I'd been doing the same job in industry, my wages would have soared, whereas we received an absolute pittance. But people don't go into politics for the money, and I got my rewards elsewhere. I'd bump into people who'd say, 'Oh Frances, thanks very much, we got everything fixed. That door's been hanging off its hinges for a long time, but a man came the day after I went to you.' When people stopped me in the street, that was my satisfaction. I'd walk through the town centre with a bit of pride.

I'm not trying to make out that I was the be-all and end-all, but I always made myself available. Some people came to me with tiny problems that I wouldn't consider seeing a councillor about, but I realised that they were feeling burdened and wanted someone else to take over the worry. They didn't know who else to turn to. I loved every bit of it – the surgery, the meetings, the committees. And along the way I earned myself a reputation for being a bit of a comedienne.

· 9 ·

Family Life

Life hadn't stood still during those early years of local politics: the family had continued to have its share of ups and downs. In 1970 my mother had a stroke. She was seventy-two, and she had been going out with the handcart since starting work officially at the age of twelve. She moved in with my sister Nellie, and her memory began to slip. 'Who's your mother? Do I know her?' she'd ask. It must have been really difficult for Nellie – it was hard to see someone so strong, so full of humour and compassion, stumble into confusion, and think that actors on the television were people she'd known in her youth, and that money was missing from her pension. After all those years of toil, she died without a halfpenny, and we couldn't even get any assistance towards her funeral because my dad hadn't paid enough stamps when he was alive. Nellie was appalled, but I told her, 'They did nothing for Mam during her life; let's not worry about them doing nothing now she's dead.'

A year later, Michael's father died. Grandad Clarke died suddenly, which made Michael's shock all the greater. He'd been a great ally of Michael's, always on his side when he was a young lad, whatever bother he got into. His death, so soon after my mam's, felt like the disappearance of their generation: they'd endured such hardship, but they'd always kept their dignity, and now they were gone.

Fortunately, in 1972 there were two causes for celebration. We were offered a larger house, and accepted with alacrity. With eight children, Mick and me, our three bedrooms were groaning at the seams. We moved to a four-bedroomed semi, where we've stayed to this day. Just before the house came up, I'd booked a holiday – which was to be the very first time Mick and I had been away alone since 1948. We set off for a week at Butlin's in Pwhelli, Wales. I think we had only two days of good weather, but we enjoyed our first break and there were plenty of opportunities for laughter. I recruited some fellers to join Mick in a barber's quartet – 'Mick's Grill' – who came third in their competition. I didn't fare so well in the quest for 'Lovely Legs' – I didn't even reach the first twenty. That caused some consternation. 'How many years have we been married,' I challenged Mick, 'and you've been telling me a lie?'

I must have overcome my sense of outrage, because 1973 was our twenty-fifth wedding anniversary. I wanted to have a party, but the cost seemed prohibitive. Rene said, 'Book the scout hut and we'll see how many people want to come, and we'll all pay £2.' The scout hut was an ideal venue because it was on the periphery of the estate, so you could stay as long as you wanted without disturbing anyone. I said OK. The idea was that the money we received would buy all the alcohol, the buffet and disco. The anniversary fell in between Christmas and New Year – so the party took place on the nearest Saturday. We ran around, trying to get everything on the cheap, and somehow we managed it. The women did all the work: we fetched the barrels, the pumps, the crates, every drink you could think of, and the cutlery, and we prepared the buffet to boot. The men sat back while we organised the lot; we must have been soft. But what a time we had! The party was a huge success – we were dancing and carousing until Lord knows when. In fact it was so successful that it became a New Year's ritual in the neighbourhood for years to come. The money that was made was ploughed back into the next year's do; no one made a profit. We had some cracking times, and that party became part and parcel of our culture.

There would always be some drink left over from the party, and this became the privilege of the organisers; we'd arrange a ladies' night, which was an occasion in itself. We'd go to Kathleen Dougherty's because Kathleen was divorced and could do what she liked, so we'd have a fancy dress party at her house. One woman, May, a neighbour of Kathleen's, was dressed up for the grand event, but couldn't tell her children where she was going because she knew they'd follow her. She phoned for a taxi, got into it and directed the driver down the street, round the block and back again into her own road. 'Hey, love,' he said, 'haven't I just been to your house?' May, decked out as the genie of the lamp, gave him a suitably mysterious smile. Oh how the drink flowed on ladies' nights, when we women were left to ourselves!

My children started getting married, led by our Michael, who married Balkis in a registry office. After the ceremony we found our way to their flat. They were living on the top floor, and after winding up the spiral staircase, we entered their room. It was filled with mattresses and the mattresses were filled with bodies – fellers and girls were sprawled all over them, smoking pot (at least, I think so). Mick and I picked our way in and out of the arms and legs, towards the drinks table, trying to behave as if this were an everyday occurrence for us swingers . . .

Margi married next, and then our Marion. We didn't see Marion tie the knot because things were a little fraught: we'd had an argument some months earlier. We're both very headstrong, but normally in our house arguments die down quickly – not because of my attitude, because I'll never retreat, but Mick always makes the first move to bring about peace. I think Marion takes after me in some ways – she's as stubborn as I am. Like everything else, you remember the row you had, but not its cause, although I'm sure it was about something stupid. Marion said she was leaving home and going to live with our Nellie. She was away for quite a while. At the end of the year, she announced that she was pregnant and getting married. Of course we were all upset, especially Mick, because Marion was the apple of his eye. It caused a furore at the time, but

Greg is a real gentleman and he idolises Marion.

Things weren't easy for them in the beginning. Six or eight months after Little Gregory was born, it was discovered that he was brain-damaged. Greg was stationed in Germany and it was a real struggle for Marion, being separated from her family at such a worrying time. We were all concerned for her and Frank went over to give her some support, as did Margi. That's what close-knit families are for in times of trouble.

Soon I had three grandsons: Balkis had Adam, and Margi had Lawrence. It seems funny that I'd had so many daughters, but my children were producing sons, and there was another on the way. Eileen found out that she was pregnant. Of course I was extremely upset – she was only nineteen and not at all worldly-wise. There was a lot of shouting and barging, but Mick and I had to be philosophical about it and give Eileen our help. When she went into labour, I was with her practically until the baby was born, and I was the first to hold him. Eileen named him Gerard, because St Gerard is the patron saint of expectant mothers. I was determined that although Eileen had the baby, that wasn't going to stop her from having her own life. She went back to work and I minded Gerard, until she got him into the local nursery.

Not all my political campaigns were on behalf of other people; I began one of my own. In 1976 everyone was being converted to North Sea Gas, and a company called the Press Gang (whose name caused a few laughs) were checking household appliances. A workman came to my house, took one look at my cooker and said, 'We can't convert that, love.'

'Why not? It's only twenty-eight years old.'

He was laughing, but insistent: 'I'm sorry, you can't have that converted.'

'All right, you keep the pipes there, I'll stay on the town gas and you'll have to go around me.'

Then a gas salesman came and said, 'It's time you got yourself a new cooker.'

'I'm sorry, I can't afford a new cooker. That one's perfectly good – it cooks to my satisfaction and still serves its purpose.' He couldn't get round me, but he came back the next day: 'There's a lovely reconditioned cooker in the saleroom – you'll love it. It's only £60, with a £1 deposit.'

The cooker was delivered, but as the mechanic was connecting it he said, 'I'm sorry, there's something wrong with this cooker. It's only got three legs. I'll get you another leg.'

There I was with my cooker, which was nice enough, but he didn't return with the other leg, and it had to be propped up. I kept ringing the Gas Board and saying that I wasn't going to pay for it until the new leg was delivered. My calls fell on deaf ears. Men would come to read the meter, and say, 'So much for gas and so much for the cooker.'

'Sorry, that's in dispute,' I'd reply. Every collector accepted my word. It got to the stage where I'd had the cooker for about three years and still hadn't paid more than a pound for it. But one day an argument began.

I told the gas man, 'You can't have any money for the cooker.'

'I've got to, love, it's down here.'

'You're not getting out of this house with any money. You can take money for the gas, but I've been on to them about this cooker and no one's been. I don't intend to pay until it's sorted out to my satisfaction.'

Then he rang the gas company: 'I've got a very irate customer here, Irene, and she won't give me the money for the cooker.'

I took the phone from him. The girl was very nice: 'Oh dear, that's wrong – do you want me to send someone round to repair it?'

'I don't want it repaired, I want it sent back, but please give me some time to get a replacement.' Six months later someone came to collect the cooker, but fortunately I wasn't in. Eventually I was sent a court order telling me that if I wanted to appear in person, I should complete the relevant section of the form and put 'faulty appliance' as my defence. The instruction came for me to attend court, and my friend Kathleen Dougherty said she'd keep me company. She thought I was scared, but I wasn't. The place was packed with people appearing before the judge for debt, and we listened to all the cases. The court emptied rapidly until Kathleen and I were the only two left. The Clerk of the Court approached us.

'Oh, my nerves have gone,' said Kathleen. 'What are they going to do? Why don't you plead guilty?'

'It's not a hanging offence,' I said, 'it's only about a cooker.'

The two of us were giggling and laughing, and the clerk said, 'Excuse me, madam. What was your case?'

'Frances Clarke v. the British Gas Corporation.' I spat the words out.

He told us to wait, then he came back and said, 'I'm very sorry, but that case has been withdrawn.' I said I didn't intend to leave the court until the judge had heard my case. Off went the clerk, and returned with the judge.

'Now madam, can you explain to me why you haven't paid for the cooker?'

'I've already explained to your clients, and they didn't effect the repairs. For three years I made constant requests for repairs to be made – they were ignored, so I didn't pay. Furthermore, Judge, what would you do if you ordered a Rolls-Royce and it came with only three wheels? My cooker has only three legs. Every time I make a sponge cake it's always skew whiff.'

'I don't wish to know about the three-legged cooker,' he said, but he was laughing. I think it was the only time I've felt sorry for a gas official – the judge turned to him and asked, 'What's going to happen now?'

'Mrs Clarke can pay half a crown a month.'

'I'm in this court now,' I said, 'and I'm telling you – I am not paying you one cent. You'll have to bring me back to court.'

'I have to make an order for you to pay,' said the judge.

'That's fair enough, but I'm not paying.' Kathleen and I left, and we laughed all the way home.

A few weeks later I received a letter from the Gas Board instructing me how to pay the outstanding debt. I turned over the page and wrote: 'I'm returning all these documents, as I've already stated my case in court and I do not intend to pay.' I didn't hear any more from them. And what happened to the cooker? I gave it to a pensioner, and as far as I know she's still using a cooker with three legs.

What with my young grandchildren and all my council work, life was pretty full, and I was busily moving from one moment to the next. Then, in 1978, tragedy struck once more, and everything blew apart. Marion's husband had been stationed in Nebraska. Marion was coming home for a holiday with little Greg and the new baby, Jonathan. I went down to Heathrow to meet her. Every detail of that day stands out – it will live with me for ever.

I had to go from Euston on the Underground, and I remember thinking: If our Michael was here now, he'd tell me where to go and what to do. It was about ten o'clock in the morning on Saturday 18 March. I met Marion and the children, and we headed back for the Liverpool train. There was a football semi-final on; the station was swarming with Liverpool fans, and I knew some of the young lads. At Lime Street we caught a taxi, and when it arrived home, someone opened the taxi door. I remember getting out, and seeing lots of people in the house. Isn't that nice? I said to myself – they've all come to welcome Marion home. There was my brother Teddy, our Nellie, Marie, Balkis, and Mick's brother, Patsy. I thought it was a lovely gesture, but something felt strange. Mick took hold of my arm and said, 'I've some bad news for you.' I couldn't for the life of me think what he was going to tell me.

'Our Michael's been killed on a motorbike.'

I was just stunned – I couldn't take it in. I started to scream. I became hysterical, and they sent for the doctor.

I went up to the hospital where they'd taken Michael. The Sister who'd tried to save his life was there. There are such unanswerable things that happen at moments like that. Her name was Kathleen Clarke – I thought she was our Kathleen who'd died. Michael and Kathleen had always been bound up together, so it seemed right that the last one to offer any help to him was called Kathleen Clarke.

Michael was buried with Kathleen and his grandad. Mick and I didn't realise how popular Michael was. The house was filled with his friends, and friends carried his coffin. After the funeral a group of them came back to our house and sang all the Beatles' songs. Michael would have liked that.

His life was cut short, just like Kathleen's. I tried to find solace, but I couldn't. Mick and I were devastated. I said, 'Our Michael was such a strong personality that if there's anything beyond life, he'll let us know.'

I didn't realise that he'd let us know quite so soon. Three weeks later I went up to bed to be by myself and weep. All of a sudden, I felt a presence beside me that was so strong my hands reached out to try and touch it. I knew it was Michael. It was about half-past ten and, comforted, I fell into a deep sleep – my first since Michael had been killed. At midnight, Mick woke me. His mother had died at half-past ten. Michael had idolised Grandma Clarke, who'd more or less reared him, so that was his way of letting me know.

The rest of the year was like marking time. With the deaths of Kathleen and Joan, I'd had the comfort of my religion, but with Michael there was no comfort to be had from anything or anyone. I felt desolate. All I wanted to do was to be by myself and scream. I refused to go to church, but my friend Mary persuaded me to join a three days' retreat at Upholland Seminary, in Lancashire. I thought that it was going to be a time of seclusion, a space to rid myself of bitterness by being alone, but that was not to be. The first hour was silent, but thereafter we were taken to a classroom for a course in Christianity. It reminded me of school, with sheets of paper laid out on desks, and I felt reluctant to participate. I knew, however, that I'd be seen as stand-offish if I didn't contribute. Gradually, I started to come out of myself, slipping back into my sense of humour and telling jokes and stories to the others in the group.

At the end of the retreat I felt stronger, and began to come to terms with the grief I was nursing. Nothing can mitigate my loss of two daughters and a son, but since then I've tried not to let bitterness and hatred take hold of me. I'm by no means a goody-goody though. Sometimes I rant and rave at home – Eileen calls me the War Department, and I certainly declare war!

· 10 ·

The Brezhnev Years

Margi and Frank both had theatrical ambitions and I encouraged them to attend the Eliot Clarke School of Drama and Dance, which gave them confidence and poise. Margi appeared in various plays and secured a part in the Granada production 'What's On', where she presented the region's television programmes. She was about twenty-three, with flaming red hair, and made everyone gasp with some of the statements she came out with. She told Demis Roussos, 'You look as if you've swallowed a couch.' Frank tried for various parts, but he was a little too self-conscious and writing, rather than acting, was his forte. He sent scripts and ideas to all kinds of producers and wrote several episodes for *Brookside* in its early years. One way and another, Margi and Frank found their different footholds in the profession.

In 1983 Frank finished the screenplay of *Letter to Brezhnev*, and sent it around to see if any company was interested; no one seemed to be. He was getting despondent, but then he found a way to put it on as a play. People loved it. Mick said, 'I don't like our Margi using all that bad language.' But I told him, 'Margi hasn't used any; it was Teresa, the person she plays. Did Tony Curtis's mother or father think he was the Boston Strangler? She's just playing a part.' After that, Mick looked at it in a different light.

The silence from the film and TV companies was still depressing Frank, and it was a demoralising time on Merseyside – unemployment was raging, and the Toxteth riots erupted. Frank felt that he met a brick wall everywhere he turned. Then Fate took a hand. One of the Greenham Common campaigners came to Kirkby, but couldn't find anywhere to stay because she had two large dogs. Frank's an animal lover, and as he totally admired the Greenham cause he said that Fiona Castleton could stay at his flat. Within a week of her visit she wrote to Frank, inviting him to her house on the Isle of Man. Frank was unemployed, so his mates threw a few bob in the kitty, Margi threw a few bob in, and so did I.

If this was a film, nobody would believe what happened next – but it's true. Frank was astounded when he arrived at the house. It was magnificent: the Castletons were wealthy; their business was Baxi fires. The family were interested in *Letter to Brezhnev*, and said they would back it. Somebody else said they'd put money in, and the whole thing snowballed from there. The budget started off at £50,000, but in the end the film cost about £350,000. But that's nothing – it's only the tea bill on some of the films that are made now.

Things started to buzz. *Brezhnev* was the first film made about Liverpool by people who know the score. It was made on a shoestring, but people took the story to their hearts and willingly gave their time for little money. Alfred Molina and Peter Firth worked their socks off for something like a fiver a day; Margi and Alexandra Pigg also threw their souls into the film. It was a wonderful opportunity for local talent *and* for family and friends. I was one of the women waving enthusiastically in a scene at the dockside; our Angela was in the film too. She'd already appeared in *Brookside* as Damon's first girlfriend and, young as she was, was beginning to carve out her own career as an actress.

Everyone pitched in and put their all into *Brezhnev*. Some of the scenes were shot at Rene's house, and she treated the film crew as if they were family. When they were shooting outside in Kirkby, they'd all come to our house in between takes. The place was packed. The budget couldn't run to a catering caravan, so I'd make everyone a butty or some soup. They were all welcome.

It was an incredibly heady time, and it was even more exciting when the film was in the can and ready for distribution by Palace Pictures. There was a premiere in Kirkby, and everyone turned out for a fantastic party that night.

Soon the acclaim for *Letter to Brezhnev* began, and reviews started to pour in. Some people were offended by its bad language, but I think that those who were had closed their ears to the real message of the film and the vision of Liverpool it portrayed. The BBC phoned to ask if Joan Bakewell could interview us for 'Newsnight'. Not one of the Clarke family is camera-shy; we were all excited by the thought of meeting the famous personality, and Eileen and I cleaned the house with a fine toothcomb in preparation for her arrival.

She was lovely, warm and sincere, and we gave her our usual welcome. The programme gave a real boost to the film.

Brezhnev was a huge hit locally – it was on at the Liverpool Odeon for six months – and nationally it became a cult film. Margi and Alexandra did a lot of promotional work, travelling to Canada and the States, and appearing on chat shows.

In January 1986, Margi and Alexandra were told they'd won a BAFTA award for the best newcomers. The ceremony was to take place at the Savoy Hotel in London, and Frank and Margi booked a room for me and Mick. This was something else we never ever thought we'd do – stay at the Savoy for the weekend. It was an experience I'll never forget, although I tried to walk in as if it was a natural, everyday event. In the evening, I wore a lovely black dress and Mick had his dicky bow on. We were done up like dogs' dinners. Margi looked fabulous. At the reception, we met all sorts of people – Jeremy Isaacs, Anthony Andrews, Jeremy Irons, Twiggy, Sally Ann Field, George Harrison, and Barry Norman, whom I thanked for his reviews of *Letter to Brezhnev*.

The whole thing was an extraordinary experience, and I loved every minute of it. It didn't change my life – I'd still be down the shops with my trolley – although I revelled in the occasions when people realised that Frank and Margi were my kids, and would come up and tell me how well they'd done. My only sadness was that Kathleen and Michael weren't there to share their glory: Michael would have charmed the birds off the trees and Kathleen would have had a businesslike influence on them. For Frank and Margi, *Brezhnev* was only the beginning. Frank's made two more films – *Fruit Machine* and *Blonde Fist* – and Margi has done the TV series *Making Out* and *The Good Sex Guide*, but there was something very special about the making of *Brezhnev*.

During 1986 my health started to waver. I've suffered from eczema since Kathleen took ill – at one stage I'd have my hands bandaged for up to six weeks at a time – and when Michael was killed, it came back with a vengeance and attacked my feet as well. I kept going to the doctor and the doctor kept saying I had arthritis, but it wasn't that sort of pain; I knew it was circulation. I had X-rays and all sorts of examinations, but nothing picked up the problem.

One weekend, when Frank was staying, I was in terrible pain with my left foot. He took off the bandage and said, 'I'll tell you what, we'll go to the hospital.' I went along just to please Frank. I explained to the nurse how I'd had no sleep all night and felt ill, then sat down to wait for my name to be called out. While I was sitting there, I decided to have a fag. I smoked about forty or fifty a day, and during the night. Something told me that I wouldn't smoke again.

A young doctor gave me a full examination from head to toe and said, 'I need the registrar to have a look at you.' She wouldn't let me walk, but put me in a wheelchair. The next thing I knew, I had an electro-cardiogram all over me. The registrar asked me if I smoked and I could see him looking at me with disdain, as much as to say, 'You stupid woman.' I was arrogant – I'd always thought: No one's going to stop me smoking – but he said, 'Well, I'm telling you now, you can never smoke again.'

I had gangrene. I haven't smoked from that day to this. The medical attention and nursing care I received was second to none. I had to have major bypass surgery to save my leg – I was right: the arteries were diseased through smoking. The moral is: DON'T SMOKE.

· 11 ·

The Hillsborough Disaster

In April 1989 a tragedy struck Liverpool that ricocheted throughout the country: the Hillsborough disaster, when so many young lives were lost. It's appalling how an occasion for celebration – Liverpool's place in the FA Cup quarter-final against Sheffield Wednesday – so swiftly became a scene of devastation.

I'd been shopping on the afternoon of 15 April, and on the way home I asked someone, 'How's the match going?' 'Oh, there's been trouble,' the woman said. 'It's terrible, someone's been killed.' Oh my God, I thought. Liverpool and Everton fans have always been renowned for their good behaviour, and I hated to think of anything happening that would allow the press to tear Merseyside to pieces. Back at home, Mick greeted me with the news that there had been a tragedy, and that nine or ten people were dead. It was about four o'clock in the afternoon, and the news was coming through in dribs and drabs; the implication seemed to be that there had been a fight. None of us could make any sense of it.

There was a knock on my door, and the daughter of

a neighbour and fellow councillor appeared. 'Frances, my dad's in Sheffield. We've kept trying to get through on the phone. My mum says that if you try as well, maybe one of us will hear something.' I stood by the phone for the next two hours, hoping that Billy was all right, but all the lines were engaged. I then started phoning friends, and anyone I could think of, trying to get news. In the meantime, the death toll was rising.

I ran round to Vera's to see if she'd heard from Billy, but she'd heard nothing and was completely distraught. It seemed that the only thing to do was to go to Hillsborough, but just as I was preparing to leave, Billy phoned. He'd been in a different part of the football ground and he was safe; he hadn't even known of the tragedy the other side of the pitch. We were so relieved that we all wept.

A heavy gloom had settled over the area, and no one could talk about anything else. All voices were subdued – the whole of Merseyside waited. No sooner was I home than Rene called to ask if I'd go round to her daughter, Irene, whose husband Alan was missing. I dropped everything and ran. Irene had gone to Sheffield, but Alan's mother, Sadie, and his brother were there. We got through the evening, and it was just before one o'clock in the morning that Irene phoned to say that Alan had been killed. Before the news came through, we'd had to get a doctor for Sadie, and fortunately, he broke the news to her. My heart went out to Sadie – I know what it's like to lose a child.

On the following day, there were some terrible articles in the newspapers: the tabloids had gone to town. On the Monday, there were yet more shocking photographs and features about Liverpool fans, more or less implying that they'd deserved all they got. The *Sun* carried some appalling accusations which were later found to be totally untrue. Everyone was outraged – people were calling the local radio stations and the BBC and weeping, and the radio stations condemned the *Sun* and the *Mirror*. The *Mirror*'s editor said that they'd been wrong, and would retract their stories, but the *Sun* said no such thing – they maintained their position.

We didn't know what to do – we couldn't believe that insults were being heaped upon people's grief. It seemed indecent and inhuman. I was talking about it with my family, and suddenly I decided what to do. 'Eileen, we'll make a placard.' I went into our garden (where there's all sorts of rubbish hanging around) and found two poles from sweeping brushes, and two pieces of wood, and we knocked them together. Eileen did the wording, in large bold print on coloured paper. It was something along the lines of 'Don't buy the lies of the *Sun*'.

'I'm going over the town centre with this,' I said, 'and I'm going to organise a protest.'

'I'll go with you,' said Margi, who was visiting at the time.

'I'm not getting the bus,' I said. 'We'd miss half the people. We've got to walk from here.'

I walked with Margi – of course I did feel self-conscious, but I was determined that we should make a protest one way or another. As we were walking, people began to fall in behind us. *En route*, I sent someone into the unemployment centre for a loud-hailer. By the time we reached Kirkby town centre there must have been about forty or fifty people with us, and as we walked through the town, with me shouting through the hailer, the numbers grew. People surged round – the place was absolutely jammed tight, and the mood was furious. Someone bought a copy of the *Sun*, and we burnt it, then a cry went up: 'There's *Sun* reporters here.' If one had been found, I'd have felt sorry for him. One reporter said he was from the *Liverpool Echo*, but people were shouting: 'No, he's not.' Feelings were running high. It had been my idea to march, so I didn't want any trouble. I had to keep a tight rein on everything. Luckily, the reporter said that Margi could vouch for him, and she did.

By the afternoon, hundreds and hundreds of people were there, incensed by the injustice. The people of Liverpool had been tried by the press and found guilty, but the fans had done nothing wrong. They'd simply tried to rescue people who were being crushed to death. Some of those lads are still traumatised, as are the parents and grandparents who lost the fifteen youngsters. We protested for a week, persuading people not to buy the *Sun*, and newsagents not to stock it. We organised a picket of newsagents from six to eleven o'clock in the morning and, although he's not an extrovert like me, Mick joined the line because he felt so deeply about the whole thing. Not everyone refused to buy the paper – some bought copies as an act of defiance because they didn't want to be dictated to – but by and large we were heavily supported. The fund-raising for the victims' families drew an enormous response as well; people really gave generously in sympathy.

Sales of the *Sun* plummeted, and I don't think they've ever fully recovered from that campaign. I was accused by the owner of orchestrating the protest as a politician. That was utterly untrue. It wasn't politics, it was because my friend's son-in-law was killed, and lots of youngsters alongside him. We were being unfairly lambasted, and I wanted to put a case forward for Merseyside and for the victims. I was to relive the tragedy of Hillsborough when I attended the unveiling of a statue, erected in their memory, as Mayor of Knowsley. Of all my duties, that was the most traumatic.

· 12 ·

The Mayor of Knowsley

Throughout the 1980s, I'd continued to sit on the council. Elections were held every four years, and every time I increased my majority. I think that's because of my approach: I'm relaxed about talking to people and I don't stand on ceremony; they'll call me 'Frances' rather than 'Councillor Clarke'. I tried to help where I could, and a lot of help's been needed: the Tory government has decimated Merseyside and demoralised the community. In the mid-1980s I was asked if I'd consider being Mayor of the Kirkby borough of Knowsley, but I was heavily involved in my council work, active on the Education Committee and Chair of the district. The time didn't seem right.

In 1991, Stan Kelly was appointed Mayor and his wife Pauline was to be his Mayoress. He was a dedicated man, and our political sympathies coincided; I was really pleased for him. But before Stan could take up his position, he had a heart attack and died. We were all shattered – his death was completely unexpected. Some weeks later the leader of the council, Jim Keight, asked me if I would be Mayor.

I hesitated and said I'd think about it over the weekend. Everyone at home thought that I should say yes. I'd been in politics a long time, and served the community to the best of my ability – not always successfully, but in the best way I could. When I'd made my decision, I spoke to Pauline's daughter Lynn and asked if she thought that her mother would be my Mayoress. I thought it would ease her grief a little, because she'd be so busy for twelve months, she'd be exhausted. Pauline agreed, so I phoned Jim to say that I'd love the job.

My forthcoming appointment was announced in the local newspapers. Shortly before the big day, I went into the town centre with my shopping trolley, and some people I knew stopped me and were taking the mickey, curtseying and tugging their hair.

'Well,' I said, in my grandest manner, 'none of you needs to do that. Today I'm like you, a nonentity. And until the 22nd of May I'll be a nonentity, but after the 22nd I'll be someone, and you'll still be nonentities. Good afternoon.'

I walked away. I hadn't gone more than ten yards down the pathway when they started laughing hysterically: the bloody wheel had fallen off my trolley. 'There's someone up there taking *you* down a peg or two,' I thought. 'You'd better behave yourself as Mayor.'

In May 1991 Pauline and I were duly appointed. It was a fantastic day, a day I'll always remember. The ceremony went smoothly, and my speech – more or less made off the top of my head, as ever – was well received. We celebrated in the evening with family and friends, and then came Civic Sunday. The service – in my case, a Mass – must have been attended by two hundred people, whom I'd known over the years. Several council officers came as well as all sorts of people from my past – with my teachers Miss Murphy (who'd long since been Mrs Daniel) and Miss Hennersey among them. It was a real occasion.

Then it was down to mayoral duties, accompanied by a sleek black limousine, driven by George, the wonderful chauffeur, my chain of office, and the safety pins needed to keep its heavy links in place. 'Oh, you're going to cost this borough some money,' George used to laugh. 'You've never got your pins.'

By a strange coincidence, my first mayoral duty, at the League of Welldoers, took me back to my childhood.

The League was established in the 1930s by Lee Jones, a Welsh philanthropist who recognised that people dreaded going on parish relief and felt degraded by it, no matter how needy they were. He saw that they needed an occupation to give them pride in themselves and pay them a wage, however small. He'd set men to build tunnels and do other labouring jobs, and even if the tunnels went nowhere, those men had been employed and felt that the money they received was their due. Lee Jones was loved in Liverpool, especially in the area where I lived – around Scotland Road – which saw real hardship and quite a bit of boozing and brawling. He also organised Christmas parties for the children of the district, but you could go to those only by invitation. They were provided for those whose families were really destitute. Each child was given a gift at the party, and I always longed to go to one. Every year I'd stand with my nose pressed against the window, but however hard I pleaded, I wasn't allowed in. Sixty-odd years later, I was the League's guest of honour, with the Mayor of Liverpool and a judge.

The judge knew the area, and in his speech he described the terrible conditions he'd seen as a volunteer worker for Lee Jones, and how his name had been given as security against a loan when times were hard, and how difficult it was to recoup the money. He was an extremely witty speaker, and when he began to talk about the schooling in the region and the strange notes he used to receive from mothers about the facilities, everyone was in tucks. Then it was my turn.

'I'm going to give the judge a shock,' I said, 'because I also know this neighbourhood well, and those lavatorial arrangements are something I'm familiar with. He used to get notes from the mothers saying that Johnny couldn't come today because he hadn't been, but as soon as he's been, he'll come. The judge and I have something in common: some years ago he was finding it difficult to get money from people and, at around the same time, Provident were finding it difficult to get money from me. I know all about how tricky that can be. I'd also like to let you know that in 1936 I came here and couldn't get in because I didn't have a ticket. It's taken me years to get a meal here, but what a reception it's been. Today, I've been welcomed by the staff, the Lord Mayor of Liverpool, and the good judge. It just goes to show that everything good comes' – and the whole audience joined in – 'to those who wait.'

I knew I was going to be a different kind of mayor. Like others before me, I wanted to bring the dignity of the borough to the forefront, but I wasn't going to pretend to be grand just because of my title. My philosophy was that the people of the borough should feel connected with the Mayor – the role shouldn't be seen as something distant from them. If George and I were on our way to some function and saw people at a bus stop who were going in our direction, we'd give them a lift. I don't see the logic of having only one person in the back of a limousine that can hold five or six – why shouldn't others share the facilities of the borough? I'll give pensioners lifts to the bingo and tell them, 'Don't forget to let me know if you come up trumps – I'll be looking for a discount.'

Most people liked my approach, and it gave me the support of ordinary folk, but I think gestures like that marked me out as a bit unusual. Though I hadn't thought I was newsworthy, the *Sunday Times* and the *Independent* came to interview me.

Pauline and I were invited everywhere. Sometimes we went to two or three functions a day. There were luncheons and dinners, fairs, fêtes and flower shows to open, and all manner of voluntary organisations and charities to visit. I can't recall the number of times we attended services at the Anglican Cathedral and events at the Royal Philharmonic Hall. We had a full itinerary, and seemed to drive down every street in Merseyside during the year. We also travelled further afield – to the town in Germany, Stadt Moers, which is twinned with Knowsley. I'd been there some years earlier, as a councillor, and they gave me a wonderful welcome when I returned as mayor.

It was hard work, but a wonderful opportunity, and I met so many people from all walks of life. One of my favourite occupations was visiting the elderly who couldn't get out very much, and listening to the stories they had to tell. On one occasion, George knocked at a door and announced, 'The Mayor of Knowsley, Councillor Mrs Frances Clarke,' and who should be there but Miss Bentham, one of my favourite sweet-shop owners from Roscommon Street. She'd been kind to me all those years ago, and now I had the chance to do her a good turn. It's funny how things come round.

Not all the visits were heartening – I remember one man of eighty-five whose wife was in a dreadful state: she couldn't really communicate, and just spent her days sitting on a chair. He looked after her well and, rightly, was proud of that, but their flat had only the bare necessities, no comforts whatsoever, and it was so distressing that they should be in that position. Lots of moments like that upset me, but if I was able to do some good by speaking out about them, it justified the role of Mayor for me.

There were humorous incidents to offset the solemnity of that role. Once Eileen accompanied me to a drinks party when Pauline was on holiday. Neither of us had managed to have anything to eat before we left, and as there were only dainty canapés at the party, we were on our knees with hunger by the time it finished. We made George drive round and round, looking for somewhere that was open. I'd love to have seen the look on the shop owner's face when the large mayoral car drew to a halt outside and a uniformed chauffeur asked for cod-and-chips twice and then opened up the large mayoral umbrella to protect them from the rain. I think George was busy with the air freshener that night . . .

· 13 ·

Disappointment
and Triumph

My style of office was something new for the borough,
but I had considerable support from council officers
who respected the amount of work I did for the area.
At the time, I thought that everyone was on my side.
We all like to think that we're the bee's knees and are
universally popular, but unfortunately we're not. When
you discover that some people really dislike you, it's
puzzling and you try to think back and ask yourself:
'What did I do to them, to make things turn out this
way?'

In early 1992, I was advised by one of the councillors
to keep running my surgeries. The advice was unnec-
essary because I'd made sure that throughout my
period as mayor, I'd kept up with my constituency work
– talking to people about their problems and trying to
find solutions. I'd fallen down on reporting back to the
ward meetings, but there's a dispensation for that
because while you're attending mayoral functions,
you're engaged in the business of the borough. What I

hadn't realised was that while I was absent at such functions, certain individuals were plotting against me and planning to take away my seat – the seat I'd won for the Labour Party sixteen years earlier. I'd always felt that I gave value for money – not that money came into it, because councillors simply receive an allowance for expenses. But I'd wanted to do the job, it was my choice, and I felt that I'd answered the needs of the people and had support on the council. However, I'd been lulled into a false sense of security by some of the people I'd always trusted.

That was the worst part of it: the discovery that people I'd regarded as my friends, trusted wholeheartedly, and supported in the past, were working against me behind the scenes. People have to give their allegiance to the Party, not to an individual, but if someone had helped me in the way I'd helped some of them, I wouldn't have been able to do enough to repay them. My allegiance would have been 110 per cent. A little loyalty wouldn't have gone amiss, but in my case, it wasn't forthcoming. The branch (they're no longer called wards) adopts their representative, and so it came to pass that when I went up for selection and adoption, another person had also been invited to attend the meetings. Lo and behold, I lost the adoption by two votes. I thank those who gave me their support, and hope that my actions didn't embarrass them, and although I don't feel any animosity towards those who voted against me, I couldn't comprehend their reasoning, and still don't understand how I offended them. I'm not an angel, and sometimes I can say things that hurt people without realising it, but I've never knowingly done anyone an ill deed.

I was absolutely shattered by the decision, and because no one told me where I'd gone wrong, my defeat was even harder to swallow. I felt numb with shock, but I didn't cry, I just went home to my family. They were as devastated as I was, because they knew I'd done my job, and couldn't be criticised on that front. I didn't do my council work only in the school where I took my surgeries, I did it in the town centre, in the library, at Kwiksave, at bingo, and at home in the evenings when the telephone or the doorbell rang. Everyone had my phone number: wherever I was, if people wanted help, all they had to do was ask. Back home, the phone started ringing and friends, neighbours and people from all over the ward called to say that they just couldn't believe what had happened, especially during my mayoral year. The whole thing seemed unbelievable.

The next few weeks were punctuated by the sound of the telephone and the hope that I'd be able to make a swift comeback by becoming the candidate for Kirkby Central, but those hopes were dashed, and my immediate political future within the Labour Party looked bleak. In the past, I'd criticised people who'd left the Party and gone Independent, and although I felt shattered by my deselection, I didn't intend to follow suit. A number of letters were sent to the *Liverpool Echo*, the *Kirkby Challenge* and the *Star*, all of which had covered the story, objecting to what had happened, and I received personal letters from some of the papers, expressing their disappointment. The people of

Whitefield Ward itself decided my fate. A couple of supporters in particular swayed my view. Jimmy Dunn wrote to the *Challenge*, saying how concerned and disgusted he was, and in the town centre I bumped into a local woman, Mrs Mallo, who said, 'Oh Frances, I'm really upset by what's happened. Who are we going to turn to now?'

That evening I sat at home, mulling over what had happened and trying to work out what to do for the best. I'm a Labour Party supporter through and through, from the cradle to the grave – nothing will change that – but I was incredibly disappointed by some of the things that had happened. I decided that as I wanted to continue representing the people of the ward – and they seemed to want me – I would have to stand as an Independent Labour candidate. It wasn't a move against the Party, but for the ward. The first person I rang was Rene. I felt it my duty to let her know what I was going to do. Although I knew she'd be upset, I explained the reason for my action, and Rene listened. She wouldn't condemn me (she only ever condemned the Tory Party) because we went back a long, long way, through hardships, happiness and sorrow. She was disappointed, but she didn't criticise, and I think Rene knew what had been going on behind the scenes. I then informed the leader of the council, who was disappointed because I'd be outside the Party rather than making a contribution within it. He tried to talk me out of it, but I was determined. Once I'd made up my mind, I was going to go through with it come hell or high water. My third call was to Paddy Shennan of the *Echo*; I thought it courteous to let him know. Then all hell broke loose.

There was a concerted effort by everyone concerned to have me ousted, but the people of Whitefield really came up trumps. They knew the dilemma I was in, and some of them were absolutely wonderful – they rallied round immediately. Emily Scott and her husband Jim, a solid trade unionist, were appalled by what had happened, and told me, 'There's no way we're going to vote for anyone else but you. You've given us what we want, you've given us hope when there was none. Things have been done that we've been asking for for years, but were never looked at until you took them up.' Comments like that really gave me a vote of confidence – they were like a battle cry. I knew that there were pockets of people who knew my intentions were sincere, and were willing to help me.

My friends Mary Amos, Kathleen and John McNulty and Billy and Vera White also leapt to my support. Billy became my agent. A small printing and stationery outlet had been set up at Roughwood School to help promote Kirkby, so I went there to get my leaflets printed. They helped me with the format and presentation of the leaflet, which looked magnificent. It explained all that I'd done in the past and what I hoped to achieve in the future, and some people said that I gained their votes because they were impressed by the presentation of the leaflet. A lot of people helped me, and we canvassed hard from dawn to dusk. On one occasion, I started talking to a woman who had no idea who I was, and at the end of our conversation she said, 'I've really enjoyed talking to you. I've always been a lifelong Tory, but I'm going to vote for you.'

On the day of the election, Margi, Frank and Jane were real troupers. The polls shut at nine o'clock, and with about ten minutes to go they were still out and about, coaxing people to vote. All the family and friends turned out. It was a ding-dong campaign.

The count took place at Kirkby Suite, and I paced the floor while the votes were totted up. When Whitefield Ward was called, I was summoned for the announcement: 814 votes for me and 600 for my opponent. I accepted the seat and thanked everyone for this vindication of my ability and loyalty. Everyone knew I was a Labour supporter – they wouldn't have voted for me if they'd thought I was anything else. People may not know the political intricacies within branches and constituencies – I don't know them myself – but they know who they're voting for and why. They knew that when I was on the council or in committee, I spoke for the people, in their language, not in the language of a seasoned politician. I spoke as they wanted me to speak and highlighted the things that needed to be done in the borough. It was like that all the way along the line. It's always been like that. After my triumph, there was a carnival atmosphere at home. We really had a ball, and the phone didn't stop ringing all night long with messages of congratulations.

My victory took place in May, as my mayoral year was drawing to a close, and there was a further surprise ahead. It's been customary for the departing Mayor to enjoy a year as Deputy Mayor after handing in the chains of office, but the council decided to reverse this tradition, in order to allow a lead-in period for future mayors. I think this is a good idea, but it meant that I wouldn't have the benefit of the role of deputy, nor indeed would Harold Campbell, my successor. Still, I'd had a good run of functions during the preceding year, and one of my last official duties certainly gave me something to remember.

Pauline and I visited Dallas, Texas, where I'd been invited to accompany a group of young Knowsley footballers (though, thankfully, not to play). When I discovered that our trip would take us only an hour's journey from Azle, Michael's old haunt, I couldn't resist the temptation to visit the Whites. We'd kept in touch over the years, albeit intermittently, but I'd never set eyes on the couple who'd done so much for my son. When we arrived in Azle, I was told they'd left town and my heart sank, but luckily their new home was only a short distance away. Pauline and I set off for a drive down a road that was little more than a dirt track and when I saw the house ahead of me, I realised that time hadn't been kind to the Whites. I was to discover that they'd both suffered with ill health and that the cost of treatment had forced them into pinched circumstances.

As soon as I introduced myself as Michael's mother, Mr and Mrs White began to weep. I quickly joined in, and as the three of us hugged each other and cried, Pauline began to weep too. Mr White spoke of Michael as a lad of great courage and his wife felt sure that our meeting was meant to be. I wouldn't have missed that strange and joyous afternoon for the world. As we said our goodbyes, they gave me a portrait of Michael that Shirley Crabtree had painted. It was a good likeness and a generous parting gift, for they'd loved Michael and treated him as if he was one of their own.

I had different tears to contend with when I was introduced to the Mayor of Azle. A man appeared before me, looking as if he'd just stepped out of the cinema screen. 'Good day, Ma'am,' said this cowboy in his late seventies, complete with stetson, spurs and holster, 'I'm Cy Rone.' I bit back my laughter and presented the Mayor with a clock – a gift from Knowsley – and said a few words to introduce myself. He seemed rather embarrassed by the gesture as he had nothing to offer me in return and turning to the police chief at his side, suggested that I was taken on a tour of their municipal buildings.

It doesn't take long to inspect a one-horse town but I made the right noises as I was shown the fire engine in its shed and the adjacent police station, where I warmly greeted a young girl, before realising from the look on the police chief's face that I was fraternising with a prisoner! When we returned to the Mayor's office (two doors away), I saw that someone had hastily picked some hedgerow flowers and placed them in a drinking glass to make the room look more worthy of my 'official' visit. 'Now Ma'am,' said the Mayor, ceremonially placing a cup in front of me, 'I'm afraid I can't offer you this special cup,' – it was decorated with steers' heads – 'but I'm going to do something nice for you.' With a great flourish, he produced a flask, half-filled the cup with water, and dipped a tea-bag in it. I don't think I've ever found it so difficult to keep a straight face.

· 14 ·

Epilogue

If I were to describe all the events of my life, I'd need to write a book the size of *Gone with the Wind*. These pages only cover its highlights – I've many more stories to tell. My only sadness is for my family and friends mentioned here who have passed away. May they rest in peace.

We remain a close family and although several of my children no longer live in Kirkby we're constantly in touch with one another. I also have ten lovely grand-children who keep me on my toes. Mick and I are approaching our 45th wedding anniversary, so I think that another 'do' is in order!

Controversy still follows me. I intend to protest against the medical incinerator that is being built in Kirkby and against the closure of a Catholic school in Whitefield, and I'll continue to speak out on any issues that threaten people, especially those in Kirkby.

THE 4-VOLUME AUTOBIOGRAPHY OF KATHLEEN DAYUS

'We must be thankful that Kathleen Dayus has survived to tell her story so movingly and so well'
– Jeremy Seabrook, *New Society*

'An evocation of a vanished world as vivid, moving and spiced with humour as any I have read'
– Hazel Leslie, *Sunday Telegraph*

'It is a privilege to share her life' – *Good Housekeeping*

Kathleen Dayus has become a legend in her own lifetime. Born into the industrial slums of Birmingham in 1903, she left school at fourteen and started writing at the age of seventy. The indomitable spirit, humour and sheer verve that characterise her life shine out from these marvellous memoirs. Nobody has captured 'her people' with more vitality, wisdom and wit. This extraordinary autobiography – written in the splendid tradition of Flora Thompson's *Lark Rise to Candleford* and Helen Forrester's *Tuppence to Cross the Mersey* – is as evocative as any written this century.

HER PEOPLE
Winner of the J.R. Ackerley Prize for Autobiography, 1983

WHERE THERE'S LIFE

ALL MY DAYS

THE BEST OF TIMES

Also by Kathleen Dayus

THE PEOPLE OF LAVENDER COURT

'Yer got some big ideas, Annie, but I carn't see any better future for any of us around this Godforsaken 'ole. We've bin born 'ere an' I suppose we shall die 'ere like our parents an' their parents . . .'

The people of Lavender Court: Aggie, orphaned at ten whose life is to see violent changes of fortune; Florrie, the good-hearted neighbour whose feckless daughter throws two households into scandalous uproar; and Annie, daughter of Aggie and Fred, who manages to carve out a life of some dignity. Frank and unsentimental, Kathleen Dayus takes us into the slums of turn-of-the-century Birmingham – a harsh world made bearable by kindness, courage and laughter.

Inspired by the stories told to her by Annie Green, whom Kathleen Dayus met in a community home, the author of *Her People* once again deservedly wins our admiration and love as one of the most compelling storytellers of our time.

THEY TIED A LABEL ON MY COAT

Hilda Hollingsworth

'[This] passionately lived book is wonderfully evocative of its time, funny and sad . . . written from the courage of the soul' – Dirk Bogarde

Hilda Hollingsworth was just one of thousands of evacuee children to leave London at the beginning of the war in 1940. Her brilliant evocation of those childhood years – gritty, searing and rumbustious by turns – is as richly entertaining as it is heart-rending.

As the bus pulled away from the school playground, it was the last ten-year-old 'Ild and her young sister Pat would see of their mum until the war's end. Shunted hither and yon to 'places of greater safety', their final stop was the harsh Welsh mining village where the children were picked over 'like a blooming cattle market', and where life was redeemed for 'Ild by her dauntless, loud-mouthed friend Winnie. Separated from Pat and banished to the smilingly sadistic Joneses, 'Ild was tormented by their cat and mouse games. The fire and brimstone Williams offered some solace, but next came the redoubtable Auntie Bron . . .

OUR JOYCE
1917–1939
Her Early Years

Joyce Storey

Set in the pre-war Bristol of corset and chocolate factories, of 'service' and glamorous silent movies, *Our Joyce* is about school, the first job, the first love and a sorrily mismatched marriage – all told with a brilliant eye for the comic in the tragic.

JOYCE'S WAR
1939–1945

Winner of the Raymond Williams Memorial Award

With an RAF husband rarely on leave, Joyce, the mother of two girls, fights her own battles on the homefront – with air raids, in-laws, machine work and poverty – searching always for her dream house and a life to call her own.

Joyce Storey, born near Bristol in 1917, began her autobiography at age 66. Destined to join the ranks of Laurie Lee's, Helen Forrester's and Kathleen Dayus' autobiographical classics of the twentieth century, *Joyce's War*, the sequel to *Our Joyce*, evoke in marvellously vivid colours, the ordinary story of an extraordinary working-class woman's life.